LONG-TERM ATHLETE DEVELOPMENT
TO IMPROVE PARTICIPATION AND PERFORMANCE IN SPORT

FUNdamental • Learning to Train • Training to Train • Training to Compete • Training to Win • Retaining

Administrators • Athletes • Coaches • Officials • Parents • Performers • Players • Teachers

sport Northern Ireland

Youth Sport Trust

NCSS

sport wales
chwaraeon cymru

sports coach UK is the brand name of The National Coaching Foundation and has been such since April 2001.

ISBN: 978-1-902523-70-5

Series Editor: Istvan Balyi

Author: Ian Stafford

Based on material by Istvan Balyi et al in his work on
Long-term Athlete Development

This resource has been developed in partnership with colleagues from Sport England, Youth Sport Trust, **sport**scotland, Coaching Northern Ireland, Sport Wales, Sports Council Northern Ireland, National Council for School Sport, Somerset Activity and Sports Partnership, Padiham St. Leonards Church of England Primary School and the National Coaching and Training Centre, with specific thanks to Graham Ross, Andy Martin, Clive Brewer, Paul Whitten, Ian Blackburn, Robin Gregg, Craig Handford and Roger Davis for their contributions.

All photographs © Alan Edwards unless otherwise stated

Published on behalf of **sports coach UK** by

sports coach UK
114 Cardigan Road
Headingley
Leeds LS6 3BJ
Tel: 0113-274 4802 Fax: 0113-275 5019
Email: coaching@sportscoachuk.org
Website: www.sportscoachuk.org

Patron: HRH The Princess Royal

Coachwise Ltd
Chelsea Close
Off Amberley Road
Armley
Leeds LS12 4HP
Tel: 0113-231 1310 Fax: 0113-231 9606
Email: enquiries@coachwise.ltd.uk
Website: www.coachwise.ltd.uk

sports coach UK will ensure that it has professional and ethical values and that all its practices are inclusive and equitable.

90685:2

Preface

The role of the sports coach has never been more important. Coaches play a key role in helping to develop people that reaches beyond the confines of the football pitch, tennis court, swimming pool or athletics track. The well-being of individuals, communities and the nation can be promoted through sport. Sport is valued as an important tool in addressing key social issues such as health, anti-social behaviour and racism, and in helping to create more cohesive communities.

The Government recognises that coaching is central to the development of sport at every level.

Department for Culture, Media and Sport, 2001

For sport to be effective as a vehicle for positive social change, coaches must ensure that participants are given every opportunity to:

- experience achievement
- fulfil their potential
- develop positive attitudes
- adopt a healthy lifestyle
- enhance their self-esteem
- develop their confidence.

As a coach, you must appreciate that responsibilities are associated with the wider importance given to your role. Sport has the potential to provide the most rewarding and fulfilling of experiences that can promote positive individual development, but only if presented and structured appropriately.

Increasingly evidence from research has led many sport organisations to examine some of their past competitive structures and training practices and review how young people are developed in sport. A high-quality, school physical education programme can introduce and develop an appropriate variety of relevant skills that will encourage and help children to participate in a wide variety of activities. Lifelong sport has a vital part to play in developing these skills and associated attributes.

In some sports, young people participate very competitively in their early teens and then drop out shortly after. Although a variety of reasons have been put forward for this, there is a strong suggestion that dropping out may be related to the way young people are developed **in** and through sport. Clearly, a logical, progressive approach to developing young people in and through sport is necessary, whatever their aspirations may be.

Long-term Athlete Development (LTAD), based extensively on the work of Istvan Balyi, is one of a number of approaches that focus on key, common principles of individual development, which has helped sport organisations to consider good practice in long-term planning for young athletes.

This resource aims to set out the key principles, stages and components of LTAD, while highlighting key implications for coaching.

❝ THE GOVERNMENT RECOGNISES THAT COACHING IS CENTRAL TO THE DEVELOPMENT OF SPORT AT EVERY LEVEL. ❞

Department for Culture, Media and Sport, 2001

Contents

Introduction

Many governing bodies of sport are adopting a more systematic approach to developing participants called LTAD[1], much of which is based on the work of Istvan Balyi. This is intended to produce a long-term approach to maximising individual potential and involvement in sport. For many years, high-quality coaches have been working with high-level performers, but one of the central messages to emerge from LTAD is the importance of having high-quality coaches working with children and young people during the early stages of their involvement in sport.

Although a primary aim of LTAD is to produce greater numbers of performers who are capable of achieving at the highest level, it also provides a platform for coaches to encourage and support participants at every level to fulfil their potential and remain involved in sport. Only a relatively small number of coaches will work with elite performers. The emphasis in this resource, therefore, is on promoting principles of good coaching practice that are associated with both improving individual performance and promoting the benefits of lifelong involvement in sport. There are key messages here for 'participation coaching', where there is more of a recreation orientation and activities are normally carried out in more informal and less structured environments, and 'performance coaching', which is more directed towards improving those athletes who are engaged in developing within performance-oriented, competitive sport. sports coach UK is currently working with a number of recognised experts to evolve the Participant Development Model (PDM) and the Coach Development Model (CDM). Examples of these can be downloaded from www.sportscoachuk.org

For those coaches who do work at higher competitive levels, the guidance relating to the later *Training to Compete*[2] and the *Training to Win*[3] stages should be of particular interest. However, the principles, processes and practices that relate to the first three stages must be appreciated in order to place the overall preparation of competitive performers in context. The LTAD model provides a structure for developing individuals and outlines the key coaching principles and practices that relate to the various developmental stages through which individuals progress.

ALTHOUGH THE TERM *ATHLETE* IS USED, THIS MODEL IS NOT JUST ABOUT PARTICIPANTS IN TRACK AND FIELD ATHLETICS. THE TERM IS INTENDED TO COVER ALL PARTICIPANTS AND PLAYERS/PERFORMERS IN SPORT WHO ARE REQUIRED TO DEMONSTRATE 'ATHLETIC' ATTRIBUTES AND SKILLS.

> Coaches should remember that the principles and guidelines set out in this resource are central to an evolving and flexible approach to developing sporting capabilities. They should not be viewed as rigid rules – coaches coach people! If a real participant-centred coaching system is to be developed, training, preparation and competition programmes must account for individual differences.

[1] See pages 7–18.
[2] See pages 39–43.
[3] See pages 43–47.

1

General principles of good practice are identified throughout this resource. However, these may be modified over time in response to scientific findings and the empirical evidence of coaches, or on the basis of individual coaches' professional judgements about the appropriateness of certain aspects for the participants they coach.

The key principles that characterise this LTAD model are:

- It takes approximately 10 years of extensive practice to excel in anything; if potential is to be realised, there are no shortcuts.
- The nature of the growing child and the early stages of development must be a central consideration when planning and implementing coaching programmes.
- Differences in the nature of sports, whether they require young people to specialise in them at an early age or later, are key to determining training and competition programmes.
- The fundamental skills and *physical literacy*[1], gained during a child's early sport experiences, in subsequent development, are vitally important.
- *Windows of trainability* that appear at different times during maturation should be paid particular attention. If these windows are fully appreciated and exploited, the training effect will be optimal and will significantly help true potential to be realised.
- Young athletes' competitive and training programmes should be reviewed. This might involve more innovative and creative thinking from coaches as well as restructuring of competitive experiences. Coaches are challenged to consider what they can do and what they can influence.
- Involving a whole range of significant other people such as parents, teachers, administrators, fixture secretaries and officials, in order to produce an integrated and progressive sport experience for young people, is necessary.
- Striving for *system integration* or *pulling it all together* for the athlete, in terms of sport experience in schools and clubs, coaching programmes, coach education, competitive structures and appropriate support systems, is a key requirement.
- Committing to continuous improvement is important. The LTAD model should reflect good coaching practice in terms of being constantly reviewed and improved in the light of research evidence and changing environments.

[1] See pages 7 and 17.

Continuous improvement is at the heart of this LTAD model; it is evolving and will be constantly reviewed and progressed as appropriate.

Effective coaches are coaches who constantly reflect on their practice and beliefs (*heads-up coaches*). As a coach, do you simply coach as you were coached (*head down*) or do you:

• understand why you do what you do?
• reflect on how effective your coaching programmes and sessions are?
• seek new information about coaching?
• understand the importance of considering the developmental stage of an individual?
• challenge yourself to improve?

LTAD provides the opportunity for coaches and others who are centrally involved in sport to reflect on and review current approaches and methods used to develop young participants. Any opportunity for pause and reflection, to simply take stock of what we do and how we do it, must be grasped.

In the busy world of sport, it is all too easy to become a head-down coach, looking no further than the next training session, competitive event or season. For coaches to be really effective, a heads-up approach is vital, where constant reflection is the main vehicle through which continuing improvement is sought.

Throughout this resource you will be challenged to stop reading, lift your head up and reflect on these questions, as well as how you will apply LTAD principles to coaching delivery.

This resource provides coaches with relevant knowledge and understanding that should help them support participants at every level – from the school playground to the Olympic podium. Topics covered include:

• the key elements of the LTAD model
• physical literacy and its value in enhancing long-term participation and performance
• key development stages within LTAD relating to participation and performance
• key components of athletic performance
• approaches to developing sporting talent
• implications for coaching, coach education and development.

1.0 WHAT IS LTAD?

FUNdamental • Learning to Train • Training to Train • Training to Compete • Training to Win • Retaining

Administrators • Athletes • Coaches • Officials • Parents • Performers • Players • Teachers

1.0 What is LTAD?

This chapter outlines some of the key elements in the present LTAD model. If coaches see excellence as a relative, personal term – being as good as **you** can be – then there is no conflict between developing people at the participant level and producing high-level performers.

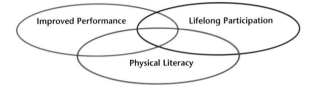

Figure 1: The fundamental role of physical literacy

In its more general sense, the term *physical literacy* is used to imply a child's competence in the full range of fundamental movement skills that underpin subsequent acquisition and development of more specific life and sport skills. However, in the context of LTAD, coaches should assume that physical literacy also implies mastery of fundamental sport skills. This issue is addressed again later.

It is acknowledged that the promotion of a systematic approach to developing performers in sport is not a new concept. Recently, the work of Istvan Balyi on LTAD has come to prominence, focusing the thinking of coaches and administrators in sport into viewing the development of sporting talent in a much wider context. It is acknowledged that a few key approaches to the development of talent have contributed to the present LTAD model[1]. The current LTAD model within the UK is illustrated in Table 1 on pages 21–22.

1	2	3	4	5	6
FUNdamental	Learning to Train	Training to Train	Training to Compete	Training to Win	Retaining

1 Build overall movement skills

2 Learn all fundamental sports skills

3 Build the engine and consolidate sport-specific skills

4 Fine tune the engine, skills and performance

5 Maximise performance, skills and engine

6 Adjustment/retain players/athletes for coaching/administration

[1]Refer to the *FHS* articles listed on page 65 for further details.

Happy accidents?

There are many examples of performers who come late to a sport, or sometimes almost by accident, but still achieve at the highest levels within that sport.

A recent example is that of a 16-year-old schoolboy with no real interest in sport who was spotted through the talent identification and development procedures operating within rowing. His potential was identified through a battery of tests conducted at his secondary school and he embarked on a programme of accelerated learning and development within the sport. One year later, he achieved a silver medal in the National Junior Championships and approximately two years later, aged 18, he won a silver medal at the World Junior Championships. Rowing is a sport that does not depend on early specialisation and is relatively well suited to this sort of late transition, but this is indeed a remarkable achievement in such a relatively short time frame.

> Coaches should reflect on the following questions.
>
> Do athletes succeed because of a system or in spite of it?
>
> Is success at the highest level due more to good luck than good management?
>
> Although there may be many more individual examples of such *happy accidents*, surely the more systematic approach to identifying and developing talent that has now been adopted in many sports should produce a more progressive, integrated and effective system.

The 10-year Rule

It takes 10 years of extensive practice to excel in anything.

**Dr Herbert Simon
(Nobel Laureate and Professor of
Computer Science and Psychology)**

A key LTAD principle identified previously, is the suggestion, based on scientific research, that it generally takes 8–12 years of training and preparation for a talented performer to reach the highest levels.

This belief contrasts sharply with some coaching practice that emphasises winning at an early stage in a performer's development as being of overriding importance. This approach is often referred to as *peaking by Friday*, where the coaching and preparation programme is dominated by the, often weekly, competition schedule. Coaches know that performers must dedicate themselves to long-term preparation programmes in order to achieve their true potential. This needs to be not only reflected in their coaching programmes and practices, but also communicated and emphasised to performers, parents, administrators and other coaches.

Coaches will be well aware that an individualised and well-planned training, competition and recovery programme will support optimum development throughout an athlete's life in sport. Opportunities to achieve and succeed in sport at any level, will be improved through a long-term approach to preparation and performance, rather than any short-term emphasis on winning at an early stage. Everyone associated with an individual's attempt to achieve their full potential while striving to reach the top level, must understand that this pathway has no shortcuts. If any aspect of a performer's development is not given adequate time or support, there may always be some shortcomings in vital skills or attributes.

A short-term approach to developing participants will be equally ineffective in attempting to keep more people involved in sport for longer. If fundamental movement skills are emphasised and developed in a systematic manner, participants at the earliest stage should be:

• better equipped and more confident
• more willing to try a range of sports
• more able to make successful transitions to other sports
• able to find at least one sport that captures their interest
• more motivated to make sport a continuing part of their lives.

Early- and Late-specialisation Sports

In terms of differing training requirements, sports can be broadly categorised as either early or late specialisation. Examples of early-specialisation sports include gymnastics, diving, figure skating and table tennis. The nature of these sports, in terms of developing high-level performers, demands a much earlier sport-specific specialisation in preparation programmes. Most sports, with a few notable exceptions, are late-specialisation sports. In these sports, a more generalised approach is beneficial in the early stages of development. In these early stages of late-specialisation sports, the most fundamental movement skills should be developed alongside a basic technical and tactical awareness involving a range of activities/sports.

The stages for late-specialisation sports have already been identified, but it is useful to review them alongside the recommendations for early-specialisation sports. Currently, the stages and progression for early- and late-specialisation sports within the LTAD model are as follows:

Early Specialisation	Late Specialisation
1 FUNdamental	1 FUNdamental
2 Training to Train	2 Learn to Train
3 Training to Compete	3 Training to Train
4 Training to Win	4 Training to Compete
5 Retaining	5 Training to Win
	6 Retaining

To date, work by sports coach UK has led to a revision of the stages in the table on page 9 in the form of the PDM. The first three stages are now referred to as *Active Start, FUNdamentals* and *Learning to Play and Practice*. For further details about the PDM and an explanation of these and the other stages, visit www.sportscoachuk.org

All models of good practice and approaches to the long-term development of athletes must be reviewed constantly. This may result in changes to accommodate different needs and information gained from scientific research. This is the case with the current LTAD model and this approach will no doubt continue to evolve with other models being proposed that complement or even supersede it. This is why the LTAD model described in this resource, along with others that have been, and will be, proposed, should not be viewed as a rigid set of rules. Rather, coaches should view it as a framework of principles and progression that specific sports, individual coaches and performers can apply to their own particular context.

Such models should continue to be an important focus for reflection and discussion, rather than simply be accepted and adhered to without critical examination.

As identified earlier, the focus of most of the work on LTAD has been on its potential and use with late-specialisation sports. This is because there are many more late- than early-specialisation sports, and a generalised approach would be inappropriate for the latter[1]. In terms of early-specialisation sports, it is recommended that each one develops a specific approach tailored to its particular structure and requirements. To produce a *one size fits all* model would be inappropriate as any such model would be too simplistic and would ignore sport-specific issues. It is suggested that coaches and administrators in early-specialisation sports should attempt to combine the *FUNdamental* and *Training to Train* stages. In relation to late-specialisation sports, it is recommended that there should be no specialisation before the age of 10 years, as this may lead to a lack of balance in overall development, burnout, dropout and withdrawal from training and competing.

An approximate age range is associated with each developmental stage. **It is really important that these are seen simply as rough guidelines and not precise, rigid rules.** Participants, whether children or adults, recreational players or high-level performers, should progress as and when they are developmentally ready and not simply because they have reached a certain age. To highlight this, examples of the age ranges used in specific sports will be provided.

---

[1] Gymnastics has recently developed a high-performance LTAD model and is currently in the process of developing a community-based LTAD approach, focusing on developing FUNdamental movement skills and and physical literacy for the general sporting population.

The individual stages identified within the LTAD progression for late-specialisation sports will be explained in later chapters of this resource. An age range is specified alongside each stage, as chronological age is commonly used as a basis for classifying children and young people in sport. Typically, the interaction of experience and maturation influences the development of the musculo-skeletal[1] and neuromuscular systems[2], which enable children's movement skills to improve with age.

It is useful to view the development of movement skill coordination as *related to*, rather than *determined by*, age. This will be obvious to coaches working with young athletes, as any group of similarly aged children will demonstrate significant variation in their capabilities in relation to learning and performing sport skills.

> Coaching is certainly informed by science, but coaches' experiences and *know-how* will also help them decide when and how a performer is ready to make the transition to the next stage of development.

The issue of identifying the current developmental stage of performers is addressed at various stages throughout this resource. Before setting out the implications for the individual stages of the LTAD model, it is useful to examine general principles and issues relating to training during childhood and adolescence, specifically in terms of developing fitness components and skills.

It should now be common knowledge among coaches, that classifying young performers based on chronological age is not a particularly effective approach for safe, fair and motivating competition, or as the basis for planning and implementing development programmes. Children of the same age can demonstrate a wide variation, not only in terms of their physical and movement skill development, but also in terms of their psychological, social and emotional development. To avoid the problems that might arise from an inappropriate training or competitive schedule (eg because a child is a late developer or an adult model has been applied), it would be ideal if the developmental phase of young performers could be established. However, no acceptable, viable and reliable procedures are currently in operation.

---

[1] The complex system that includes the bones, joints, ligaments, tendons, muscles and nerves.

[2] The brain controls the movements of skeleton (voluntary) muscles via specialised nerves. The combination of the nervous system and muscles, working together to allow movement, is known as the *neuromuscular system.*

Similar ages but different stages

It is recommended that, before the peak height velocity (PHV)[1] period, chronological age may be used in setting out training, competition and recovery schedules, and there is no real reason why boys and girls should not train together.

1.1 Optimal Windows of Trainability

The LTAD model has the potential to help coaches plan individualised development plans with due regard to sensitive, critical periods in maturation and trainability. A training effect may be achieved at any time throughout the various developmental stages, but it is thought that, during these specifically sensitive and critical periods, or *optimal windows of trainability*, accelerated adaptation can be demonstrated, given appropriate training loads in terms of volume and intensity (see Viru, 1995; Viru et al, 1998; Rushall, 1998).

These *optimal windows of trainability* relate to physical and movement skill development. Although these critical periods have implications for the physical conditioning aspect of a participant's development in sport, coaches must not lose sight of other key aspects of maturation, such as the stage of an individual child's social and psychological development. All aspects of individual development must be considered when planning programmes and individual sessions, so that opportunities to achieve are optimised and participants can gain maximum benefit – physically, cognitively, socially and emotionally.

[1] PHV is a rapid increase in height, often related to the *growth spurt*.

The success of any LTAD system relies on the involvement of coaches who:

• understand children
• appreciate how a child's overall development influences participation and performance in sport and physical activities
• can relate to, and communicate with, children.

How much do you understand and appreciate children and their development as it relates to your coaching? For further information on child development, coaches are recommended to refer to the sports coach UK 'Coaching Children and Young People' workshop and its accompanying resource. For further information, visit www.sportscoachuk.org

1.2 Developing Key Performance Components

This section provides an overview of the general principles and considerations relating to the five key components of athletic performance:

• Endurance
• Strength
• Flexibility
• Speed
• Skills.

Further details on the development of these components are provided in Appendix A on pages 67–69. Relevant, specific aspects of the components in relation to the key development stages for late-specialisation sports are discussed in this chapter.

1.2.1 Endurance

Before puberty, it is common for young performers to improve, mainly in relation to the efficiency of their movement skills. This means that, because they become more skilful movers, the energy cost of activity will decrease without an increase in maximum oxygen uptake ($\dot{V}O_2$ max). Young performers' $\dot{V}O_2$ max increases significantly after the onset of PHV and tends to peak between the ages of 12–15 years (girls) and 14–16 years (boys). The $\dot{V}O_2$ peak for boys demonstrates an increase of approximately 150% between the ages of 8–16 years. During this period, non-weight-bearing activities prove useful in helping to prevent injuries, particularly those related to overuse.

Accelerated adaptation within the aerobic system (peak aerobic velocity) can be related to the onset of PHV. Training programmes designed to improve the aerobic system of 10–14-year-old girls and 12–16-year-old boys need to be tailored to individual needs or, for practical considerations, they could be grouped with similar young performers for fitness work after the onset of PHV. To achieve optimal benefit, the training of the aerobic system must be appropriate to biological maturation and not necessarily chronological age. This is because young performers may be anything up to four or five years apart in maturation terms in their early teenage years.

Training groups based on whether performers are demonstrating early, average or late maturation patterns could be formed. Where this is the case, there is a better chance of effective, beneficial adaptation taking place. If all young performers at any particular chronological age are subjected to the same training programmes, there is a greater likelihood of optimal benefit being achieved by only a portion of the group, with others experiencing the detrimental effects of either under or over-training. When coaching team sports, it is recommended that squads train together when working on technical and tactical skills, but that fitness training should be determined by maturational needs.

In relation to the holistic development of performers, coaches should remember that separating young participants totally from their chronological peers might have detrimental effects on subsequent social and emotional development.

How do you presently group the athletes you coach? Does it vary depending on the activity?

heads up

1.2.2   Strength

Improvements in strength are possible during pre-adolescence or before PHV, but it seems that young participants at this stage are trainable in terms of relative strength (percentage improvements) rather than absolute strength. Introducing strength training at an early age can be achieved using fun activities with appropriately weighted medicine balls and Swiss balls. In addition to improving general strength and power, such activities should also help to enhance fundamental movement skills. Exercises, such as gymnastic activities, which make use of the performer's own body weight, are helpful in increasing strength. These fun activities used in training at the very early stages should focus on core stabilisation, as well as the stability at key joints such as shoulder, elbow, knee and ankle. Improving core stability is obviously fundamental to training throughout development.

Before puberty, strength gains will occur through physical and neurological adaptations, improved coordination and exercise. At this time, short-term strength training does not appear to impede endurance activities. It is recommended that strength training should not exceed 30 minutes at any one time and that two or three sessions per week are needed. For girls, the period that is most relevant for accelerated adaptation to strength training programmes is towards the end, and immediately after, PHV. For boys, the critical period is 12–18 months after PHV.

A current issue for coaches is the role of free weights and Olympic-style lifting techniques with young performers. Previously, many influential sports organisations, including governing bodies of sport, recommended that this type of training should be avoided at a young age. There is now increasing evidence that impressive performance gains can be achieved with young athletes through sound, carefully monitored and progressive strength training programmes that use free weights[1]. If the techniques used to lift free weights safely and effectively are seen as an extension of fundamental gymnastic movements, then good background experience in gymnastic activities should prepare young performers well for a specific free-weights programme. Coaches should keep an open mind, making informed judgements based on their interpretation of information from relevant research, literature and attendance at workshops. They should also know their limitations and should not attempt to plan or implement a programme that involves young performers lifting free weights unless they, or the personnel in charge, are suitably experienced and qualified. This issue is revisited in a later chapter on the *Training to Train* stage[2].

1.2.3   Flexibility

Work to develop optimal individual and sport-specific flexibility can be undertaken at the earliest stages in training. Monitoring the flexibility of performers is very important during, and immediately after, PHV. This procedure should be seen as an integral part of the regular screening of physique in relation to periods of accelerated growth. It is recommended that static stretching and more dynamic mobility activities should be emphasised before PHV. In addition to such activities, proprioceptive neuromuscular facilitation (PNF)[3] is recommended during and after PHV. It is not recommended that specific stretching activities are undertaken on rest days.

Traditional practice involved static stretching during the warm-up phase. This is yet another example of current research challenging existing practice. It has now been recommended that static stretching is not undertaken during the warm-up as it does not appear to prevent injuries. The current recommendation adopted for the latest LTAD model is that static stretching and PNF should be undertaken two hours before, or two hours after, training or competitive activities.

---

[1] See Blimkie and Marion (1994), Fagenbaum et al (2001) and the National Strength and Conditioning Association (www.nsca-lift.org) for further details.

[2] See pages 33–38.

[3] An advanced form of stretching, which is potentially dangerous. Expert instruction is vital to avoid damage to the muscles, connective tissue and their attachments. PNF normally requires either the coach to work with the performer, or performers to work with each other in flexibility training.

1.2.4   Speed

Two critical periods for accelerated adaptation to speed training have been identified. For girls, these are between the ages of 6–8 years and again from 11–13 years. For boys, these are from 7–9 years and again between the ages of 13–16 years.

The notion of peak speed velocity (PSV) comprises:

• linear and lateral speed (eg sprinting and changing direction)
• multi-direction (eg criss-cross, patterned drills and speed)
• segmental speed (eg leg and arm speed).

The first critical periods that are identified for boys (7–9 years) and girls (6–8 years) relate to central nervous system (CNS) development, rather than energy system training. Whereas both the volume and duration of training loads are very low, it is necessary to challenge the CNS and, to some degree, the anaerobic alactic power system[1] (eg less than five seconds of effort focusing on speed, agility and quickness with a full recovery). It is only during the second critical periods identified that anaerobic alactic power and anaerobic alactic capacity[2] interval training should be initiated (eg during intervals such as between five and 20 seconds).

1.2.5   Skills

The critical period for accelerated adaptation to movement skills and the development of coordination is called *peak motor coordination velocity*. It is generally agreed that, for boys, this period occurs between the ages of 9–12 years and for girls from 8–11 years. It is important to note that, if fundamental and basic sport-specific skills are not developed sufficiently by about 11 or 12 years, young athletes are unlikely to reach their optimal potential. This is one of several key recurrent themes that are highlighted at appropriate points throughout this resource.

---

[1] The Anaerobic Glycolytic Energy System relies on the breakdown of glycogen stored in the muscle to provide energy for limited periods (2–3 minutes) of high-intensity work. Lactate is produced as a metabolic intermediary, which leads to muscle fatigue if allowed to accumulate.

[2] The point at which lactic acid begins to quickly accumulate in the blood is known as the *anaerobic threshold* or *lactic threshold*. Lactic acid build-up can be reduced faster if you perform light exercise after an intense effort.

Physical literacy is a term that has been coined to summarise the successful acquisition and development of the:

• ABCs (agility, balance, coordination and speed) of sports performance
• fundamentals of athletics (running, throwing and jumping)
• KGBs (kinaesthetic sense, gliding, buoyancy and striking with an implement)
• CPKs (catching, passing, kicking and striking with a body part).

Physical literacy is simply defined as mastery of FUNdamental Movement Skills (FMS) plus FUNdamental Sports Skills (FSS) (ie FMS + FSS = Physical Literacy).

FMS + FSS = Physical Literacy

As suggested earlier, coaches must remember that, although skills can be trained at any age, there is a gradual decline in skill trainability after 11 or 12 years. For boys, the key training windows are between 9 and 12 years and for girls between 8 and 11 years. These training windows close gradually, therefore it is strongly encouraged that skills are learnt as close to this window as possible (ie extending into early teenage years rather than late teens or later in life). Acquiring transferable skills makes it easier for participants to change and learn new activities or sports later in life.

I tried various different sports as a child and thoroughly enjoyed them all. I didn't realise it at the time, but this gave me strong basic movement skills, which helped me to develop as an international in hockey when I started to specialise in the sport aged 15.

Jane Sixsmith

A general outline of trainability is illustrated in Figure 2 overleaf. Here, the critical periods for accelerated adaptation are identified in relation to chronological ages, general and specific training ages, the separate stages of the LTAD model and aerobic and strength trainability during maturation.

In Figure 2, no arrow indicates chronological age, while arrows indicate moving scales relating to the onset of PHV. Prior to the onset of PHV and after puberty, assessment procedures can help identify training needs, taking account of the critical periods of accelerated adaptation to training. Coaches should be able to modify this generic model to suit the specific requirements of their sport.

“

I TRIED VARIOUS DIFFERENT SPORTS AS A CHILD AND THOROUGHLY ENJOYED THEM ALL. I DIDN'T REALISE IT AT THE TIME, BUT THIS GAVE ME STRONG BASIC MOVEMENT SKILLS, WHICH HELPED ME TO DEVELOP AS AN INTERNATIONAL IN HOCKEY WHEN I STARTED TO SPECIALISE IN THE SPORT AGED 15.

”

Jane Sixsmith
Former England Women's Hockey Captain

© Brandon Malone/Action Images Limited

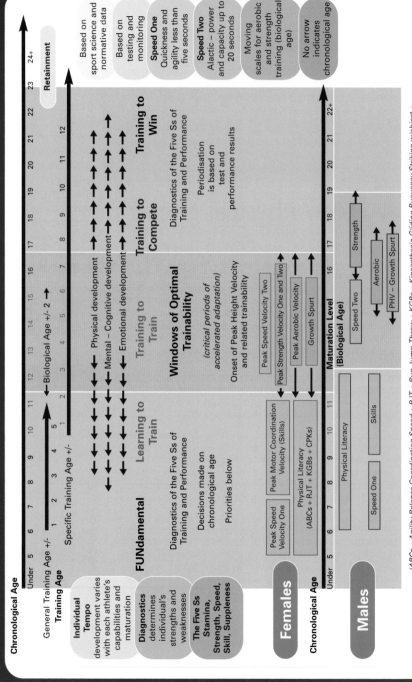

Figure 2: Adaptation to training and optimal trainability
(Balyi and Way, 2002)

(ABCs = Agility Balance Coordination Speed + RJT = Run Jump Throw + KGBs = Kinaesthesia Gliding Buoyancy Striking w/object + CPKs = Catching Passing Kicking Striking w/body)

2.0 THE LTAD MODEL

FUNdamental • Learning to Train • Training to Train • Training to Compete • Training to Win • Retaining

Administrators • Athletes • Coaches • Officials • Parents • Performers • Players • Teachers

2.0 The LTAD Model

Table 1 provides a useful summary of the key points associated with each stage of the LTAD model and shows the generic stages for late-specialisation sports. These also relate to the general phases of development for most sports. The stages will be explained in greater detail in the next chapter[1]. Coaches will appreciate that all ages indicated can only be approximations because of the wide variation within individual development.

The first three stages, with their respective approximate age ranges, are generally appropriate for all late-specialisation sports. In the final two stages (*Training to Compete* and *Training to Win*) age ranges will vary from sport to sport. A reminder of this and examples of these variations will be provided as an introduction to these stages.

Table 1: Summary of LTAD stages

Stage	Approximate Age Range (Years)	Key Points
FUNdamental	6–8 (girls)/ 6–9 (boys)	• Need to sample a wide range of movement activities in fun, playful and creative environments • No sport-specific specialisation – a multi-skills approach to be adopted • Emphasis on development of basic movement skills, not formal competitive events • Parents involved and supportive, encouraging participation in as many different activities as possible • Speed, power and endurance developed using fun games and challenges • Opportunity for optimum development of speed • No periodisation and lots of FUN!
Learning to Train	8–11 (girls)/ 9–12 (boys)	• Begin to introduce basic skills and fitness to preferred activities • Start to reduce number of sports/activities, but recommend at least three • Focus on mastery of basic sport skills through regular practice in fun-based environments, using discovery learning • Emphasis on learning to train and practise, not on performance outcome, but element of appropriate competition introduced (eg 25% of training programme).

Training to Train	11–15 (girls)/ 12–16 (boys)	• Individualised programmes based on individual development • Progressive development of technical, tactical and mental capacities • Squads split into groups of early, average and late maturers for physical conditioning and fitness work • Girls and boys may or may not train together depending on nature of activity • Regular height checks to identify key periods for appropriate training and optimum benefit • Regular, but appropriate and sensitive, medical monitoring and musculo-skeletal screening **(care must be taken here as bodies are changing and young people may be very sensitive)** • Excessive, repetitive weight-bearing aerobic activities should be avoided.
Training to Compete*	15–17 (girls)/ 16–18 (boys)	• Focus on diagnosing individual strengths and weaknesses for selected event/position and devising programme accordingly • All-year-round training that is high in intensity and specificity • Structure of training activities should simulate realistic variety of competitive event conditions • Key support structures, such as those relating to fitness, psychology and nutrition, are individualised and integrated • Performers strive to win at carefully selected competitive events, but emphasis on learning from those experiences, rather than only on winning.
Training to Win*	17+ (females)/ 18+ (males)	• Assumes all relevant capabilites have been developed • Focus of training on optimising performance or peaking at specially selected competitive events • Importance of planned rest breaks to avoid burnout and injury • General training decreased, but significant increase in sport-specific training loads • Multi-periodisation approach developed.
Retaining	Varies depending on the individual and the sport	• Performers take up alternative activities after withdrawing from competitive sport (eg coaching, administration, mentoring, other sports/hobbies, competition at masters level) • Performers should consider *training down* if used to competing at a high level.

* Coaches are reminded that these two phases will vary from the general guidelines according to the sport and the needs of the athlete.

3.0 KEY STAGES OF LTAD

FUNdamental • Learning to Train • Training to Train • Training to Compete • Training to Win • Retaining

Administrators • Athletes • Coaches • Officials • Parents • Performers • Players • Teachers

3.0   Key Stages of LTAD

3.1   Stage 1: FUNdamental

Generally:	boys 6–9 years; girls 6–8 years
Specific sport examples:	rugby union under 7–29
	girls' football 6–9 years

This stage underpins all aspects of an individual's subsequent development in sport and physical activity. Some participants may want nothing more from physical recreation than an opportunity to socialise and stay healthy. Other individuals may gain real benefits and satisfaction from competing at club level, while some performers have a real desire to progress and achieve at the highest levels. Whatever path the individual takes, the benefits of a good grounding in fundamental movement skills cannot be overestimated.

All developmental stages should be well structured and retain an element of fun, but these two qualities are particularly relevant to this stage. Progressing basic movement skills through well-structured, fun activities and games will lay sound foundations on which subsequent, sport-specific skills can be developed. At this stage, children should be encouraged to participate in a wide range of activities. This should enhance their physical literacy and their capability to undertake long-term, sport-specific training programmes.

Coaches working at this stage must understand general principles and issues relating to children's growth and development, and the implications for their programmes. They must appreciate how individual variations in growth and development should be considered when planning and coaching. In short, it is vital that coaches know about how children and young people develop, as well as their specific sport. For example, it is important to appreciate that the differences between boys and girls in terms of growth and development is minimal at this stage, so any separation of boys and girls must be justified on other grounds.

Coaches must also have a sound grasp of the relationship between the activities they undertake with children at this stage and the physical education curriculum the children experience at their primary schools. Knowledge and understanding of the approach, the activities covered and time allocations within schools should lead the coach to a greater appreciation of how activities in and out of school time can complement each other. Useful examples of coaches working in partnership with schools and teachers are provided at the end of this section and the next.

3.1.1 Guidelines for Coaches

The development programme should be fun, well structured and regularly monitored, but there is no need to plan a systematic, periodised preparation and competition schedule. The school year can provide a focus around which programmes can be built, with multi-activity holiday courses being a valuable addition to school-based programmes (eg learn to swim programmes, dance classes, recreational gym sessions and fun-based athletic activities involving learning to run, jump and throw). Even at this early stage, some children may have one preferred activity. However, in such a situation, participation in other sports activities three or four times a week is seen as essential for subsequent development. The general principle here is that three activity sessions per week will maintain levels but young participants may need at least four activity sessions per week for optimum development. Ideally, coaches, together with parents, carers and teachers, should be encouraging children of this age to have healthy lifestyles that incorporate daily physical activity between five and six days per week.

Coaches should ask themselves:
'Do I really make an effort to get to know young children from this very early stage?'
All coaches should be saying to themselves:
'It'd be really good to show the children I'm interested in *them* and not just my sport!'

A simple question that coaches might use when working with children during these early stages is, 'what else have you done this week?'. This is such a simple question, but it should help the coach to get to know the children better, understand them and their individual circumstances. Also, the answer should provide useful information on the amount and variety of physical activities undertaken.

Within a one-hour session, a recommended practice plan may include the following elements:

• Warm-up (5–10 mins)
• Work on general technical skills, including the ABCs (15–20 mins)
• Modified games or activities with simple tactics and rules (25–30 mins)
• Cool-down (5 mins).

Even if competitive sport is not the preferred route, the fundamental movement skills developed throughout this stage should be of value in terms of future physical recreation, leisure choices, quality of life, health and well-being. In addition, participation in a range of activities helps to maintain motivation by keeping young people interested and also addresses the problem of premature burnout.

Performance Components

Specific conditioning activities for strength should involve children supporting and moving their own body weight, such as in gymnastic activities, the use of appropriately weighted medicine balls and working with Swiss balls. Exercises involving the use of Swiss balls will contribute to improving core stability and upper and lower body strength. Stabilisation around the shoulder, knee, elbow and ankle should be focused on from the very early stages.

© Lee Smith/Action Images Limited

Endurance, speed and power should be developed through the use of fun and active games. In terms of endurance, during this period, the aerobic system's trainability is good. Fun activities and games with an aerobic component are appropriate. These could involve:

* chasing games
* team relays
* running pathways round differently coloured cones
* activities involving picking up and putting down bean bags while running and responding to instructions.

Although going against traditional belief and practice, it is recommended that speed and power training is essential at this stage. Training activities to improve speed are better presented near the start of a session when the children are fresh. The volume should be very low and a full recovery should be allowed between repetitions of less than five seconds (focusing on speed, agility and quickness) with the emphasis on FUN, learning new agility moves and creativity. It is useful to include a variety of such activities in one session because of the short attention span of young participants.

Similarly, the basics of flexibility should be introduced through fun activities. It is recommended that flexibility activities are undertaken five to six times per week if this aspect needs to be improved. Two to three sessions per week will maintain flexibility levels.

© Istvan Balyi

In terms of laying the foundations of physical literacy, priority should be given to effective running, jumping and throwing activities to develop the ABCs of athletics. In addition, the KGBs and CPKs that were identified in the previous chapter will extend children's experiences, develop their skills and provide variety to help motivate and sustain participation. Hand, foot and eye coordination should be developed fully at this stage.

If coaches do not feel well equipped to develop any of these skills, they may consider inviting other coaches (eg from gymnastics and athletics) to lead, co-coach or advise during some sessions.

Only the most basic rules, strategies and ethics of sports should be introduced during this time. Coaches often have to act as officials, so it is useful to stress that, even when acting as a referee, they should still be fulfilling a coaching role – only in a different way.

Some coaches may have already experienced, or heard of, Multi Skill projects that have been undertaken within their area. These projects typically consist of partnerships between sport agencies and schools, but may increasingly involve health organisations. One such project in the south-west of England, the Somerset Activity and Sports Partnership (SASP) Multi Skill Curriculum Support Project, has achieved notable success within this *FUNdamental* stage.

The pilot project, set up in April 2003, aimed to provide multi-skill curriculum support within primary schools in the county. This initial phase of the project was based on the LTAD principle that children need to establish fundamental movement skills and basic movement literacy before progressing to sport-specific work. The results from the initial project were extremely positive. Feedback from head teachers was very good, the children improved their confidence and self-esteem and, overall, a positive experience of physical activity and sport was provided. Coaches reported real value in terms of their professional development, citing the sharing of ideas, the support they received and an unexpected improvement in the way they delivered their sessions. Another benefit was that the teachers changed their perception of what can be achieved through such an approach and a renewed enthusiasm to develop the project was demonstrated.

The second phase of the project focuses specifically on the 4–7 years age group. It aims to:

• raise confidence, self-esteem and activity levels
• provide appropriate opportunities for all abilities
• identify and support children who lack basic coordination
• support teachers.

It is interesting to note the range of partners included in this project. Initially the project involved Somerset Local Education Authority, Somerset Active Sports Partnership and School Sport Coordinators. As the project was promoted, further agencies wanted to be involved. The partners now include, Primary Care Trusts, Somerset Healthy Schools, Occupational Health, Statutory Health Authority, Community Sports Coaches Scheme, sports coach UK, Youth Sport Trust and the New Opportunities Fund. Another example of coaches having to work with their heads up in order to be aware of all the agencies that could be potential partners in this vital work with young children.[1]

Summary of *FUNdamental* Stage
Boys: 6–9 years
Girls: 6–8 years

• Incorporate FUN and participation.
• Encourage general, overall development.
• Introduce ABCs of athleticism – agility, balance, coordination, speed.
• Include basics of athletics – running, jumping, throwing.
• Incorporate Medicine ball, Swiss ball, own body strength exercises.
• Introduce the simple rules and ethics of sport.
• Include observational assessments to identify key variations in development (eg height, weight, skill).
• Do not include periodisation but use well-structured programmes.
• Encourage physical activity five to six times per week.

No specific ratios are specified, but participation in a wide range of activities is recommended.

[1] Visit www.sportscoachuk.org for further details.

3.2 Stage 2: Learning to Train

Generally:	boys 9–12 years; girls 8–11 years
Specific sport examples:	rugby union under 9–12
	girls' football 8–11 years

After the LTAD model was first applied with governing bodies of sport in England (eg swimming, netball, rugby union, cricket and women's football), the need to add a new *Learning to Train* stage was identified. The reason for adding this stage is that the sensitive, critical periods of accelerated adaptation to training, or *optimal windows of trainability*, are located exclusively within one of the stages rather than overlapping two. In the initial LTAD model proposed for late-specialisation sports, general and specific sports skills were introduced and developed during the later part of the *FUNdamental* stage and the initial part of the *Training to Train* stage. With the latest modification to the model and the introduction of the *Learning to Train* stage, there is no such overlap. This development has been supported by the governing bodies of the aforementioned sports, as it makes for a more effective LTAD approach in terms of the efficient planning of the annual, sport-specific training and competition programme.

The *Learning to Train* stage is seen as the major learning stage for basic overall sports skills because the period between the ages of nine and 12 years has been identified as one of the most important for the development of children's skill learning. It is suggested that this is the time when children are in a state of developmental readiness in relation to acquiring the fundamental sport skills that are the foundation of subsequent development in sport. The basic skills identified at the preceding *FUNdamental* stage should be practised and progressed during the *Learning to Train* stage in order to acquire the basic technical skills across a wide range of sports and activities. The *FUNdamental* stage is vitally important because, if fundamental movement skills are not practised and developed before the ages of 8–9 years, subsequent development of overall basic sport skills in the *Learning to Train* stage will be impaired. While programmes can be put in place later in a participant's life, they may not be fully developed to the same extent. However, an effective intervention programme can result in limited improvement.

Towards the end of this stage, children and parents may choose to continue within sport via competitive or recreational activities (see Figure 3 overleaf). Although LTAD aims to develop sporting talent, positive experiences within the first two stages and successful achievement of physical literacy by participants can positively contribute to lifelong physical activity.

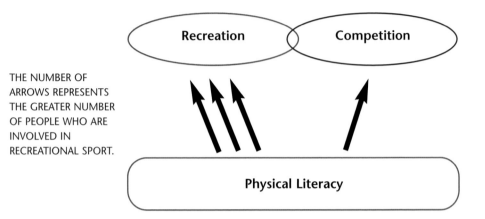

THE NUMBER OF
ARROWS REPRESENTS
THE GREATER NUMBER
OF PEOPLE WHO ARE
INVOLVED IN
RECREATIONAL SPORT.

Figure 3: Pathways within LTAD

3.2.1 Guidelines for Coaches

While young participants are aiming to do their best and win during
competitive events, coaches should be emphasising and encouraging
young participants to master the most important sport-specific skills
during this stage. This means that a much greater amount of time
should be spent on training and practices, rather than in formal
competitive events. As this is seen as the key period for skill learning,
activities that promote well-coordinated movements and basic
techniques should be emphasised. Well-structured and sequenced
training programmes should develop the other performance
components further.

There are other views about how best to structure annual training and
competition. The nature and structure of children's school life has been
considered in recommending a different pattern of periodisation, with
the suggestion that the phases of the annual plan must account for
school and family activities, such as holidays. Figure 4 (overleaf) sets out
what is suggested in relation to the volume and intensity of training and
important *prophylactic breaks*. These are the periods that provide the
necessary recovery and regeneration for young, developing athletes.
This may be an appropriate model of periodisation[1] for western cultures,
as it is more realistic in accounting for the social structure affecting the
lifestyles of young athletes and their families; more participant centred.

[1] The process of dividing your performer's/team's programme into separate
training periods, each of which will have different goals and training methods.
These periods are designed to maximise gains in the different components
of performance.

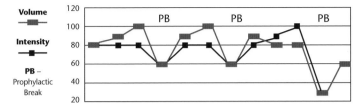

	Sep	Oct	Nov	Dec	Jan	Feb	Mar	Apr	May	Jun	Jul	Aug
Volume	80	90	100	60	90	100	60	90	80	80	30	60
Intensity	80	80	80	60	80	80	50	80	90	100	30	60

Figure 4: Periodisation for school-age children
(Balyi [1998] from Tschiene)

Finally, it has been recommended that 9–12-year-old children should participate in regular competitive events without periodising competition – this should maintain motivation. The pattern and frequency of competitions should follow the schedule dictated by the school year, accounting for the longer and shorter breaks[1].

While learning to train, young participants should devote approximately 80% of their time to training and 20% to formal competitive events, although this will vary from sport to sport dependent on specific requirements. As highlighted previously, these are only guidelines and may vary according to individual needs and the specific requirements of the sport. Also, it is useful to distinguish between the competitive experiences that young participants should be exposed to in training and the formal competitive events undertaken. It is the actual time devoted to these formal competitions that is reflected in the 20% guideline, not the competitive activities used in training. The difference between training and competing in team sports and individual sports must also be appreciated here.

A useful explanation of five stages of athlete development, combined with three forms of preparation, was identified by Platonov (1988) and is illustrated in Table 2 below. It is interesting to note that no time frames or ages are associated with the various stages of development.

Table 2: Stages of athletic preparation (Platonov, 1988)

Stages	Preparation General / Complementary / Specific			Annual Training Load (Hours)
Initial	50%	45%	5%	100–250
Basic	35%	50%	15%	350–500
Specific base	20%	40%	40%	600–800
Maximisation	15%	25%	60%	900–1100
Maintenance	10%	25%	65%	1200–1400

[1]See Balyi (1998a) for further details.

A recommended practice plan for a 90-minute session with 9–10-year-olds is as follows:

• Warm-up (10–15 mins)
• Combination of fitness and general technical skill development (20–30 mins)
• Modified or conditioned games and activities with simple tactics (30–40 mins)
• Cool-down with stretching (5–10 mins).

Among the initiatives that have been developed involving this age range, one notable success is that of a Lancashire primary school (Padiham St Leonards Church of England Primary School). The school was serving an area of high social deprivation and, before a new head teacher was appointed, it had been deemed to be educationally weak, with children lacking in confidence and self-esteem. A decision was made to start considering the children rather than the curriculum. Primary schools, like good coaches, must concern themselves with the whole child in order to help young people fulfil their many potentials – physically, mentally and socially. Physical activity and sport formed an integral part of this initiative, which included a breakfast club, aerobics, brain breaks in lessons, healthy eating and activity and two hours of high-quality physical education for each child per week.

The school believed that their Physical Education curriculum would benefit from input by suitably qualified and experienced coaches. These coaches led an in-service training day for teachers before starting the programme. Coaches then delivered the sports programme alongside the teachers for 3–4 weeks. After this time, the teachers carried on the programme by themselves. *FUNdamentals* were addressed with the 4–7-year-olds and core sport skills were covered with the 7–11-year-olds. After-school clubs were arranged to reflect the activities covered within the curriculum.

Again, effective partnerships were made with a variety of agencies and, although physical activity and sport only formed part of the strategy, one of the key beliefs was that exercise is the best *brain food* and that a child's attainment will be raised with increased physical activity. The basic skills acquired and developed through sport and Physical Education activities were seen as valuable in increasing a child's capacity to learn. Again, a reminder to all coaches that everything we do must be participant centred and that all aspects of the child's development must be considered when planning, coaching and evaluating our programmes.

This school worked hard to develop a real *child-centred* approach and it experienced the rewards that this philosophy and approach can bring. The children developed trust, pride, confidence and self-esteem. Children's behaviour improved dramatically and no child needed to be excluded for disruptive behaviour. Also, children's test results improved significantly. The school now boasts children who are happy, clean, healthy and proud. Coaches should also take pride in knowing the role they played in this initiative; they should be encouraged about the real difference that their work within sport can make to children's lives.

Summary of *Learning to Train* Stage
Boys: 9–12 years
Girls: 8–11 years

- Encourage overall sports skills.
- Recognise that this is a major skill-learning stage – all basic sports skills should be learnt before proceeding to next stage.
- Understand mental/cognitive and emotional development.
- Introduce mental preparation.
- Incorporate appropriately weighted medicine ball, Swiss ball, own body strength exercises.
- Introduce ancillary capabilities[1].
- Understand talent identification and development.
- Distinguish between double and single periodisation (although double periodisation is more common).
- If there is a favoured sport, ensure that at least 50% of the time is allocated to other sports/activities that develop a range of skills.

Training/Competition Ratio
80 : 20

3.3 Stage 3: Training to Train

Generally:	boys 12–16 years; girls 11–15 years
Specific sport examples:	rugby union under 13–15
	girls' football 10–14 years

When young participants are at such an early stage in their training development, the training year tends to be characterised by a long preparation period, followed by a transition period. If young participants compete in all available competitive events during these initial training years, this may have a lasting, detrimental effect on the development of fundamental skills and fitness. Coaches will be well aware that development could be impaired if the ratio of training to competition is inappropriate. Too much time spent on training may result in vital competitive skills not being developed as effectively, or a lack of awareness of what is involved in being totally prepared for competition, both physically and psychologically. Similarly, too much time spent on competitive events may result in fundamental techniques and skills not being developed to a sufficient standard. This may result in techniques and skills breaking down under the pressure of competition, which may have a detrimental effect on self-confidence.

---

[1] This refers to the overarching holistic components that impact on the athlete including, technical, tactical, mental, physical, personal and lifestyle.

3.3.1 Guidelines for Coaches

So, what are the recommendations in relation to planning and preparation during this stage? It is generally recommended that 60% of the time should be spent on training and 40% on formal competitive events, but these percentages will vary according to the sport and the individual. It should be emphasised that the ratio of training to formal competitive events assumes that, as in the preceding *Learning to Train* stage, young participants should experience appropriate competitive experiences within training sessions (eg small-sided games and time trials).

As with the preceding stage, when competing in events, young athletes will be striving to win, but the preparation programme should focus on developing the basic skills and understanding of the sport, rather than on the competitive events. Competition is useful in developing strategic and tactical understanding, as long as the emphasis is on the learning process, rather than on the outcome. In relation to planning and preparation on an annual basis, it is now recommended that the most appropriate structure is a double periodisation plan to keep the young athlete engaged and to maintain motivation. As identified in the *Learning to Train* stage, the principles and processes of tapering and peaking[1] should be introduced at a basic level very early on in the preparation programme. If thought appropriate, young participants can be allowed and encouraged to train through competitions, either not peaking or only implementing a minor peak. If this option is used, coaches must ensure that they communicate effectively with the athlete(s), parents and administrators so that there is a good understanding of the potential consequences. A lack of awareness here may result in any deficient competitive performance being perceived as a failure and a more negative attitude being fostered towards competitive events.

> How do you presently use formal competitive events? How do you communicate your philosophy and expectations at these events with athletes, parents and administrators?

Performance Components

The scientific basis on which coaching principles and practice are based, is subject to constant scrutiny and informed by research. In terms of current thinking, this stage is seen as fundamental to the aerobic and strength capacities for females and aerobic fitness for males. As most young athletes will probably reach puberty during this stage, PHV can act as a useful pointer in designing programmes and practices. This stage is believed to be as important as the *Learning to Train* stage for skill-based sports, such as individual and team games. As well as progressing their physical fitness and their knowledge of training principles, young athletes' understanding of relevant sports science should be enhanced.

[1] A team or performer aims to produce a training effect that will lead to *peak* performance. To prepare performers for important games or major goals, coaches will need to *taper* their training so they will peak for competition.

There has been debate about how trainable a child's cardio-respiratory system is. There is now evidence that children do adapt to aerobic training, but that they need to undertake higher intensity activities in order to achieve this. The onset of PHV contributes to the accelerated and effective adaptation of the aerobic system, which is called *peak aerobic velocity* (PAV). During this four-year stage, young participants should be grouped according to maturation levels, rather than chronological age. It is all too easy for early developers to dominate activities, especially during this stage and the following one. Coaches should constantly monitor, at least through careful observation, changes in young athletes' physique, attitudes and behaviours in order to be able to assess maturation levels. In relation to the onset of PAV, early, average and late developers should be allocated their own groups to avoid the adverse effects of either over- or under-training. Non-weight-bearing aerobic activities should dominate during this stage to avoid potential injuries.

© Istvan Balyi

How developed is a 14-year-old?

Systematic speed training can be beneficial, but coaches should be aware that adequate recovery time must be given, as work on speed endurance is not recommended during this stage. Again, a challenge to existing belief and practice is evident in relation to speed training. In contrast to the traditional sequencing of speed work, the most recent LTAD model recommends that speed training should be undertaken all year round. Within a session, it should be sequenced early after an appropriate warm-up to avoid fatigue.

As outlined earlier, strength training remains a controversial issue in coaching children and young people. From relevant literature and information obtained at coach education courses, many coaches will have understood the guiding principle to be that working with weights (especially free weights) too early, such as before puberty, is not only ineffective but also potentially dangerous. On examining such relevant literature, it can be concluded that most, but not all, of the studies identified that pre- and early-pubertal children do make similar strength gains in comparison to adolescents and adults, but that these younger children usually demonstrate smaller absolute strength gained following a training period. As explained previously, the value of working safely and appropriately with weights at these earlier stages has now been acknowledged.

There do not appear to be any adverse effects on endurance activities from short-term strength training and two to three relatively short (under 30 minutes) strength-training sessions per week are recommended. The onset of PHV is the time that is recommended as suitable for the introduction of **techniques** appropriate for lifting free weights safely and effectively because of the accelerated adaptation to strength training. Also, it is recommended that the free-weights programme is staged in relation to when athletes demonstrate peak weight velocity (PWV). The implication here is that coaches should initiate a monitoring procedure for identifying PHV and PWV.

Coaches may consider what additional training and/or qualifications they may have to undertake to better understand and complement this aspect of training or consider the use of other more suitably qualified and experienced people.

Although the underlying reasoning is sound, in that these measurements indicate more precisely the appropriate time to embark on a free-weights programme, such procedures must be thought through and handled carefully as bodily changes during this time can become an extremely sensitive issue. Remember, as coaches, we need to put the performer at the centre of all we do.

In short, strength training is an area where scientific research is asking coaches to examine their current thinking and practice. This emphasises the need for coaches to keep themselves up to date with developments in sports science and guidelines on applying this science within their specific sport.

In terms of flexibility, programming a separate, dedicated session should be considered and flexibility should be monitored carefully. It is also recommended that dynamic mobility activities are undertaken during the warm-up.

As many young people will experience rapid growth spurts during this stage, coaches may observe rather uncoordinated and awkward movements. Coaches should consider revisiting some of the key techniques and skills, and will have to exercise patience in allowing their young participants to adjust movements to accommodate their growing bodies.

Coaches need to exercise patience in allowing their young participants to adjust movements to accommodate their growing bodies and explain the potential adverse effects of this growth spurt on performance.

Also, coaches can explain to young athletes why movement skills and performance may be adversely affected at this time, so that they come to understand this as a common occurrence, which may affect many adolescent athletes during this period.

Although an overall development structure has been set out for this stage, it must be stressed that the priorities and emphasis of the training programme within each year of the stage should change according to the progress of the athlete or team. The overall pattern of change in training is characterised by a progressive move from general to specific training in the second and third years, with the programme becoming more focused on competition in the fourth year. The principles of periodisation within each year are illustrated in Figure 5. Here, the increase in specificity is influenced by the annual patterns of training. This means that specificity is always lower in the general preparatory phase (GPP) and early specific preparatory phase (SPP), but higher during late SPP, pre-competitive phase (PCP) and competitive phase (CP), as the volume of training decreases while the intensity increases. This decrease in volume and increase in intensity usually results in more time being devoted to individual and sport-specific work. Figure 5 illustrates this *Training to Train* plan and summarises how the pattern changes over the four years.

"
ATHLETES WHO MISS THIS STAGE OF TRAINING WILL NEVER REACH THEIR FULL POTENTIAL, REGARDLESS OF COMPENSATORY PROGRAMMES THEY MAY PARTICIPATE IN.
"

Balyi, 2002

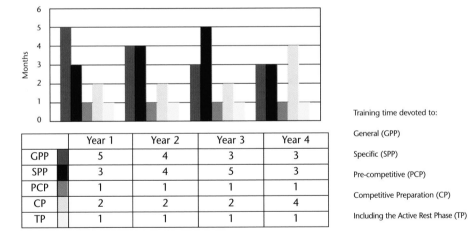

	Year 1	Year 2	Year 3	Year 4
GPP	5	4	3	3
SPP	3	4	5	3
PCP	1	1	1	1
CP	2	2	2	4
TP	1	1	1	1

Training time devoted to:

General (GPP)

Specific (SPP)

Pre-competitive (PCP)

Competitive Preparation (CP)

Including the Active Rest Phase (TP)

Figure 5: Duration of the various phases of training of annual plans within a quadrennial plan (Balyi, 1998a)

Note that, over the four years, the GPP becomes shorter, the SPP becomes longer during Years 2 and 3, but the CP becomes longer only in Year 4. In general, each successive year should evidence an increase in the individual and sport-specific content of the training programme as a sound basis for progression to the next *Training to Compete* stage.

This stage covers a particularly sensitive period of physical and skill development. Any shortcomings or omissions at this stage will significantly impair future development.

*Athletes who miss this stage of training will never reach their **full potential**, regardless of compensatory programmes they may participate in.*

Balyi, 2002

It is suggested that one of the key reasons for athletes reaching a plateau in later stages of their development is because competition was over-emphasised in relation to training during this stage.

The social and cultural education of young participants is an important aspect of overall development that should be addressed during the *Training to Train* stage and thereafter. At this stage, through the socialisation processes operating within sport, general social norms and values, along with those that relate to the sport-specific context, come to be understood. It is recommended that activities, such as cooperative games, should be used to promote development in terms of movement, cognitive and social skills, as well as emotional control. Although this may be a somewhat neglected aspect within athlete development, some sports have recognised its importance. This will be revisited in the *Training to Win* section[1].

Summary of *Training to Train* Stage
Boys: 12–16 years
Girls: 11–15 years

- Concentrate on sport-specific skills.
- Understand that this is a major developmental stage in relation to fitness (aerobic and strength; PHV is the reference point).
- Understand mental/cognitive and social/emotional development.
- Develop further mental preparation.
- Introduce free weights.
- Develop further ancillary capabilities.
- Conduct frequent musculoskeletal evaluations during PHV.
- Understand selection.
- Distinguish between single or double periodisation.
- Encourage sport-specific training six to nine times per week.

Training/Competition Ratio
60 : 40

Coaches are reminded that, in the LTAD model, the preceding three stages with their respective age ranges, are generally appropriate for all late-specialisation sports. However, the following two stages, *Training to Compete* and *Training to Win*, will vary from sport to sport in terms of associated age ranges.

[1]See pages 43–48.

3.4 Stage 4: Training to Compete

Generally:	boys 16 –18+/- years; girls 15 –17+/- years
Specific sport examples:	rugby union under 16–19
	women's football stage 1: 13 –16 years
	stage 2: 16 –18 years

As stated earlier, the vast majority of coaches work with young people at community club level, rather than with the relatively small amount who work with elite performers. The preceding three stages will be most relevant for those community-based coaches. This *Training to Compete* stage and the following *Training to Win* stage are most relevant for coaches working within centres of excellence, academies, with representative squads and targeted individuals who have been identified as potential high-level performers.

The *Training to Compete* stage aims to:

• focus on diagnosing individual strengths and weaknesses for selected events/positions and devising programmes accordingly
• provide all-year-round training that is high in intensity and specificity
• improve the adaptability of performers by structuring training to simulate a realistic variety of competitive event conditions
• maximise preparation by modelling training and competition activities
• ensure that performers' key support structures, such as those relating to fitness – including recovery and regeneration, psychology, nutrition and health needs – are individualised and integrated.

Performers should progress to this stage when the goals of the *Training to Train* stage have been achieved. The *Training to Train* stage lasts for an average of three to five years and another three to five years is required to complete the *Training to Compete* stage.

By the end of this stage, when young performers are ready to make the transition to the *Training to Win* stage, they should be adept at tapering and be able to achieve a major peak or peaks as required. To put the role of winning into perspective during the *Training to Train* and *Training to Compete* stages, performers should be striving to win at carefully selected competitive events and should be encouraged by coaches to do so. It is not so much that winning is unimportant at these stages, or that winning is somehow banned or discouraged until entering the *Training to Win* stage. It is simply that the emphasis in the second and third stages of the LTAD model is on the acquisition and development of fundamental and sport-specific skills and strategies, rather than on entering as many competitive events as possible in order to achieve short-term success. The focus is better placed on the process of learning and developing from competitive experiences, rather than on the outcome of a competitive event. This is accepted as a more effective and

healthier approach in terms of motivation, continued participation and being performer centred. Experiences gained in the former Soviet bloc countries and, more recently, in Australia, support the claim that performers who experience this structured approach perform better after the foundational stages of their preparation than others who were forced into the *Training to Win* stage during an earlier phase of their development.

In summary, adopting such an approach should be beneficial in terms of keeping more young people participating in sport for longer, benefiting fully from the experience and supporting those performers who have the ability and the motivation to progress to higher competitive levels.

3.4.1 Guidelines for Coaches

Although training to competition ratios will vary from sport to sport, the general recommendation here is that the ratio of training to competitive events and competition-specific training during this stage should change to:

- 40% of the overall time being devoted to the continuous development of fitness, technical and tactical skills
- 60% being devoted to training that is specifically focused on competitive requirements (not just competitive events, but also simulated competitive situations within the training programme).

Performers, who have progressed to an adequate level of competency in fundamental and sport-specific skills, are now exposed to activities that will develop their capacity to produce these skills under a range of simulated competitive situations during training sessions – the process of *modelling*. Programmes to improve fitness, aid recovery, enhance technical skills and psychological preparation are now individualised to focus on the specific needs of the performer to a greater extent.

A double- or triple-periodisation approach is recommended at this stage. Progressing this concept, coaches may operate double periodisation during odd-numbered years and triple periodisation during even-numbered years, which allows for shaping and varying stimuli from year to year to improve adaptation according to the demands and needs of each sport.

For further information on periodisation, coaches are recommended to refer to articles by Balyi (1998b), Balyi and Hamilton (1999b) and Bompa (1999). Full reference details are provided on page 65.

In a double periodisation annual training plan, the volume and intensity of training differ greatly from those in a single periodisation plan. With double periodisation, there is much more emphasis on individualised, sport-specific and competition-specific activities. This is a key reason why high-level performers prefer double periodisation within their annual preparation plans. After training for several years, a continued increase in terms of volume of training may present problems because of the well-documented risks associated with overtraining and overuse injuries.

This is why the intensity of training becomes the focus for the preparation and development of performers during this stage.

In relation to the current recommendation for triple periodisation, in recent years, Australian swimmers have been following a triple periodised plan with much success. Again, the plan takes account of the requirements of swimming at the highest level. Shorter training cycles allow for the achievement of three major peaks per year, at selection trials, national competition and major games (as shown in Figure 6). This triple-periodised plan is determined by the relatively short preparation period available in high-level swimming and uses a cycle of about 13 weeks, including the taper.

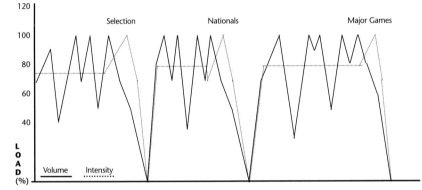

**Figure 6: Triple periodised annual plan
(Balyi and Hamilton, 1999b)**

During the *Training to Compete* stage, tapering and peaking must be addressed as a priority. As explained earlier, modelling refers to the structuring of training activities to simulate the variety of event conditions that performers may experience and is one of the key tools in developing performers with the capacity to demonstrate effective tapering. By manipulating the nature of training activities and the training environment, coaches are helping prepare their performers for all eventualities such as different weather conditions, noise levels, playing surfaces and opponents. This will help produce performers who are adaptable and not so easily distracted by any unexpected situations that may arise.

Determining the way that the training loads and competitive programmes are structured and sequenced depends on both coaching science and the coach's art. Training cycles are presented in a logical sequence that is informed by both scientific information and by the individual experiences of coaches from working within their specific sport. Where the volume is higher with intensity lower, the mesocycle[1] is longer and where volume is lower, with intensity higher, the cycle is shorter.

---

[1]Subdivisions of mesocycles, usually with a duration of between two and six weeks. Each mesocycle has a specific objective, linked to objectives of the mesocycle preceding it and following it.

When planning the structure and pattern of mesocycles, the adaptation processes of the performers' metabolisms and nervous systems are considered. In principle, the more general the training is in nature, the longer the mesocycle. When training is more specific and higher in intensity, mesocycles are shorter. The empirical information collected by periodisation experts and coaches is integral to planning any long-term preparation cycles. In addition, the distribution of cycles will be informed by: sport and exercise physiology; skill learning; hormonal adaptations; neuro-physiological aspects of training and recovery; biochemistry; and nutrition. However, the art of the coach is to use their own experiences within sport and their knowledge of the performer(s) to integrate the science and medicine into the fitness, technical, decision-making and tactical activities in producing the most effective training structure and sequence.

> For further information on the periodisation of coaching, coaches are recommended to refer to sports coach UK's *Planning and Periodisation* resource[1].

At this stage, testing and monitoring procedures should be sufficiently sophisticated to identify strengths and specific areas to target for development in relation to the key components of performance. Results from such procedures should inform fitness and skill training priorities and programmes. Coaches must be aware of the potential for interference between fitness components if two or more are being trained simultaneously. Interference occurs when the improvement in any one component being trained is reduced in relation to what would have been achieved if this area was trained on its own. From evidence to date, it has been found that aerobic training can interfere with strength training, but interference does not seem to occur the other way. At present, there is no conclusive evidence of any other interference among the components, but practical experience may suggest to coaches that problems can occur if the training of these key areas is not carefully thought through and effectively sequenced.

In summary, this stage should provide emerging performers with opportunities to prepare fully for competitive events by exposing them to a wide range of simulated, realistic, competitive conditions. Double or triple periodisation is recommended, depending on the sport and state of development of the individual. Monitoring the effects of training and competition on performers, identifying individual strengths and limitations, should help optimise development, as long as monitoring procedures do not interfere with the preparation and competition programme.

---

[1] Available from Coachwise 1st4sport (tel 0113-201 5555 or visit www.1st4sport.com).

Summary of *Training to Compete* Stage
Boys: 16–18 +/- years
Girls: 15–17 +/- years

- Involve event, position-specific physical conditioning.
- Involve event, position-specific technical and tactical preparation.
- Include sport, event, position-specific, technical and playing skills under competitive conditions.
- Encourage advanced mental preparation.
- Optimise ancillary capacities.
- Strive for full commitment to specialisation within chosen sport – 'a 24-hour athlete'.
- Distinguish between double or triple periodisation.
- Include sport-specific technical, tactical and fitness training 9–12 times per week.

Training/Competition Ratio
40 : 60

3.5 Stage 5: Training to Win

Generally: males 18 years and over; females 17 years and over – but coaches are reminded of the variation that exists from sport to sport as identified previously, for example:

rugby union: *Learning to Win* under 19–20

                   Training to Win under 20 and over

women's football: Stage 1: 19–21 years

                   Stage 2: 22 years and over

Although *Retaining* is the last stage of the current LTAD model, the *Training to Win* stage is actually the final stage in relation to the preparation of performers with the capability to achieve at the highest levels. It assumes that all of the performers' relevant capabilities have been developed and so the focus of training is on maximising performance, or peaking, at specially selected competitive events. In order to achieve this, the relevant capabilities that have been developed need to be maintained and improved where necessary. As the long-term development plan progresses, the performer's general training is decreased, but there is a significant increase in sport-specific training loads. Competitive events, competition-specific training and maintenance characterise this stage.

3.5.1 Guidelines for Coaches

The ratio of training to competitive events during this stage is 25% to 75%. The 75% of the time that is devoted to competition includes

"

THE CUMULATIVE
EFFECTS OF YEARS OF
CAREFULLY PLANNED,
IMPLEMENTED AND
MONITORED TRAINING
HAVE PREPARED
THEM TO
UNDERTAKE MULTIPLE
PERIODISATION WITH
ITS TRAINING AND
COMPETITIVE LOADS.

"

Balyi, 2002

competition-specific training activities, such as trials. Although physical and technical improvements are still possible, the most significant performance gains will come from competitive experience, modelling, tactical improvements and developing psychological skills. As in the preceding *Training to Compete* stage, diagnostic testing procedures will determine the specifics of the fitness training programme.

By this stage, some performers may have committed themselves to 8–12 years of preparation and development programmes. If this is the case, the volume of training will already be high and it would be difficult, and perhaps inappropriate, to subject the young performer to any further increases in volume. In addressing this issue for high-level performers, most sports tend to adopt a double- or triple-periodised approach, depending on the requirements of the sport and the needs of the individual performer.

For further information on this aspect of periodisation, coaches are recommended to refer to an article by Balyi and Hamilton (1999a), which illustrates phases in relation to a three-peak annual cycle and the general trends of the volume and intensity of training. Full reference details are provided on page 65.

The cumulative effects of years of carefully planned, implemented and monitored training have prepared them to undertake multiple periodisation with its training and competitive loads.

Balyi, 2002

However, in order for even superbly conditioned, high-level performers to benefit fully from these types of training loads, frequent breaks are necessary to prevent problems associated with overtraining and burnout. These breaks are composed of three to five days of active rest and should appear five to eight times in an annual plan with multiple periodisation. Achieving a balanced lifestyle may be difficult when young performers are aiming to succeed at the highest levels, but if coaches are to be truly performer-centred then encouraging balance is important.

Downhill Skiing Case Study

A detailed case study of downhill skiing is provided. Some coaches, for example, those who coach team sports, may question the value of reading a detailed example from such a sport. Firstly, please remember the value of keeping an open mind and being receptive to ideas from other sports – heads up coaching. Secondly, this is an excellent example of a real preparation programme that has been thought through carefully and designed to reflect the nature and structure of the competitive season. In short, it is a valuable lesson in problem-solving for all coaches.

An example of an annual plan from downhill skiing that identifies these breaks is presented in Table 3 overleaf.

Table 3: Annual plan 1993–94 – alpine skiing – women – downhill
(Balyi and Hamilton, 1999a)

Phase	Timing	Venue
General Preparatory Phase	May 11–June 8	Home
Specific Preparatory Phase # 1	June 9–24	Home
Sport-specific Technical Phase # 1	June 25–July 11	Whistler, Canada
Specific Preparatory Phase # 2	July 12–August 5	Home
Sport-specific Technical Phase # 2	August 6–10	Whistler, Canada
Specific Preparatory Phase # 3	August 11–26	Home
Sport-specific Technical Phase # 3	August 27–September 17	Portillo, Chile
Prophylactic Break # 1	September 18–20	Home
Specific Preparatory Phase # 4	September 21–October 8	Home
Sport-specific Technical Phase # 4	October 9–26	Hintertux, Austria
Prophylactic Break # 2	October 27–29	Home
Specific Preparatory Phase # 5	October 30–November 6	Home
Sport-specific Technical Phase # 5	November 7–15	Nakiska, Canada, Alta, USA
Prophylactic Break # 3	November 16–18	Nakiska, Canada, Alta, USA
Active Rest	November 19–21	Calgary, Canada
Pre-competitive Phase	November 22–30	Colorado, USA
Competitive Phase # 1	December 1–21	Canada/Europe
Prophylactic Break # 4	December 22–27	Home
Competitive Phase # 2	December 28–February 10	Europe
Prophylactic Break # 5	February 11–13	Europe
Specific Preparatory Phase # 6	February 14–27	Olympics
Competitive Phase # 3	March 1–April 8	Europe/Canada
Transition Phase	April 9–May 9	Home/Holidays

Table 3 illustrates a multiple-periodised annual plan for downhill skiing and acts as a useful case study in identifying key principles. These principles can be applied to any sport, but they do present a challenge to the rather more traditional and rigid plans and practices that have been evident in some coaching. The particular nature of this sport means that planning must be sufficiently flexible to integrate the physical, psychological, technical and tactical aspects of a training and competitive programme with key environmental variables. These variables include adjusting to different temperatures, snow conditions, altitude, travel difficulties (such as jet lag) and the need to produce a minor peak for technical training or for selection purposes at squad trials. In producing and implementing this multiple-periodised plan, all of these factors were considered and this integrative approach was seen as a key factor in optimising the preparation of the skiers.

The nature of downhill skiing is that there is one long competitive period (December 1 to April 8) and five sport-specific technical phases (June to November) for technical training camps on snow. To optimise this technical training at the camps, a mini-taper or minor peak was introduced to unload prior to the snow training. Overall, Table 3 illustrates that the annual plan was composed of 23 separate phases and five prophylactic breaks (PB), which included five minor peaks, one competitive period that was divided into three sub-phases, and five breaks. Within the SPP, fitness training was emphasised through activities other than skiing. During the SPPs, the lengths of the microcycles[1] were 6:1 and 5:1 to develop fitness. Immediately prior to snow training, however, the cycles were shortened to 4:1 and 3:1. Also, at this time, strength training, consisting of plyometrics and energy system training, modelled skiers' specific needs. The shorter microcycles, characterised by high-intensity work, simulated specific conditions that permitted the skiers to benefit from less fatigue and a better recovery. Skiing on snow to develop technical expertise and maintain fitness formed the basis of the sport-specific technical phase. Microcycles were shortened to 3:1 and 4:1 to ensure optimum skill development and recovery. All these measures ensured that skiers arrived at the high-altitude camp without residual fatigue that could have impaired their skill development.

The differing volume and intensity of training that the skiers will experience as they progress through the different phases is illustrated in Figure 7.

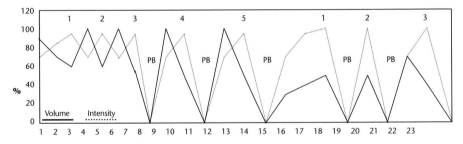

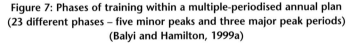

Figure 7: Phases of training within a multiple-periodised annual plan
(23 different phases – five minor peaks and three major peak periods)
(Balyi and Hamilton, 1999a)

Performers following a multiple-periodised plan can compete all year round by selecting competitive events strategically to suit their specific needs. As can be seen from the preceding examples, peaks can be achieved outside of formal competitive events, such as at training/selection camps or simulated competitions. This framework allows for a wide range of variations, but one consistent, key principle is that the plan must be tailored to the specific needs of the performers or team rather than performers being required to fit in with some pre-determined plan.

During this stage, triple or multiple periodisation is recommended, with triple periodisation being favoured for *up-and-coming* younger performers and multiple periodisation being more appropriate for the needs of established, high-level performers.

[1]Training periods of between two and 10 days in duration. They contain detailed information regarding the intensity, volume and sequence of training sessions.

A final point relates to social and cultural education and development – an issue that was raised in the *Training to Train* section. This aspect of performer development, while rather neglected, should become a focal point during the *Training to Win* stage. When training and competing at the highest levels, performers experience a variety of social, cultural, climatic and geographical conditions through their international travel. Coaches and other support staff, such as managers, can promote the socio-cultural awareness and appreciation of performers by encouraging them to experience as much of the local area and culture as their schedule will allow. Some coaches may consider this outside their remit and perhaps even idealistic. But, if we are to make any serious claims for the benefits of sport in terms of overall individual development or citizenship, then we must ensure that no appropriate opportunities are squandered. It is useful to remember the role that we have created for high-level performers as *sporting ambassadors*. Surely such performers will be more prepared and suitable for this role if they have a sound appreciation of, and are sensitive to, social and cultural issues.

Summary of *Training to Win* Stage
Boys: 18+ years
Girls: 17+ years

- Maintain or improve physical capabilities.
- Further develop technical, tactical and playing skills.
- Model all possible aspects of training and performance.
- Take frequent prophylactic breaks.
- Maximise ancillary capabilities.
- Concentrate on high performance.
- Distinguish between double, triple or multiple periodisation.
- Include sport-specific technical, tactical and fitness training 9–15 times per week.
- Consider social/cultural aspects of performer development.

Training/Competition Ratio
25 : 75

3.6   Stage 6: Retaining

This stage relates to the activities that people undertake after they have withdrawn permanently from mainstream competitive sport. Various options are open, such as staying within their sport(s) and fulfilling roles in coaching, mentoring, administration or officiating; taking up other sports or hobbies for recreational purposes or continuing to compete at masters level. This is obviously a critical stage to consider if lifelong participation in sport, with all its benefits, is to be promoted by coaches and others. Although this is not a stage that will be addressed in great detail, it is worth making a few key points.

It was reported that, many years ago, it was reasonably common practice in the former East Germany for elite performers to undertake a *training down* programme. This involved them participating in a variety of different activities and encouraging them to keep active, as well as providing advice and support on their future development. Some would argue that there should be more coordinated procedures in place to help high-level performers adjust to life without the high-level competition that has provided a focus and structure for so much of their lives. Without this structure, the excitement of high-level competition and the attention associated with success at the highest levels, it is easy to see why some performers may experience personal difficulties in adjusting, especially during the initial part of this stage.

Given the range and depth of expertise that former athletes bring with them, surely it would be of mutual benefit, for both retiring performers and sport, that a variety of options should be considered when this stage arrives. However, at present this is more of a matter for administrators and key decision-makers within sport, rather than practising coaches.

4.0 SUMMARY OF PERIODISATION AND PROGRESSION

FUNdamental • Learning to Train • Training to Train • Training to Compete • Training to Win • Retaining

Administrators • Athletes • Coaches • Officials • Parents • Performers • Players • Teachers

4.0 Summary of Periodisation and Progression

As we have now considered the first five stages in which most coaches will be involved, it is useful to consider how the quantity and quality of the training and competition programme changes as long-term plans progress. In terms of the ratio of training to competition, specific recommendations are as follows:

Table 4: Training to competition ratios

Stage	Recommended Ratio
FUNdamental	No specific ratios are specified, but participation in a wide range of activities is recommended
Learning to Train	80% training to 20% competition
Training to Train	60% training to 40% competition
Training to Compete	40% training to 60% competition
Training to Win	25% training to 75% competition

Figure 8 illustrates how a 15-year plan may be sequenced in relation to single, double and multiple periodisation. However, coaches are reminded of the latest recommendations about periodisation that have been described in the previous chapter[1]. Single periodisation appears to be less common now than previously, although some sports still retain a single-periodised annual programme as appropriate.

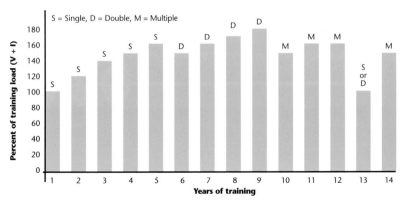

Figure 8: Integrated LTAD plan (Balyi and Hamilton, 1999b)

[1]See pages 40–43.

Figure 8 shows that, during the *Training to Train* stage, five single-periodised annual plans are undertaken to set down the foundations for future athlete development. The *Training to Compete* stage comprises of four double-periodised annual plans that should be characterised by high-specificity of training and the simulation of competitive conditions. However, coaches are reminded that triple periodisation is now favoured at this stage in some sports. During the *Training to Win* stage, it can be seen that three multiple-periodised annual cycles precede a single- or double-periodised year that represents a prophylactic or unloading year. This is normally programmed for performers immediately after major competitive events, such as the Olympic Games. This annual cycle would begin with a short, passive rest period, followed by a longer period of active rest. The four-year interval between Olympic Games has given rise to quadrennial planning. This was introduced during the 1960s and 1970s, based on the practice and success of the former Soviet countries.

> For further information on periodisation and planning a competitive calendar, coaches are recommended to refer to articles by Balyi and Hamilton (1999a and 1999b). Full reference details are provided on page 65.

Some performers may need only three single-periodised annual cycles before embarking on double-periodised training schedules. Other performers may need four or six double-periodised annual cycles before multiple-periodised cycles are introduced. In certain cases, it may not be appropriate for performers to undertake double- or multiple-periodised cycles because of the limiting nature of their genetic potential. As coaches are probably the key people who will support, advise and guide performers through the progressive stages of a training and competition schedule, a thorough understanding and appreciation of all the key aspects is required.

> When coaches work with their heads up, seeing and understanding all the implications of the big picture for the specific needs of individual performers in their sport, they are well placed to plan, implement and evaluate long-term development plans that are individually tailored and optimally effective.

> Important reasons offered for the success of the Eastern European and former Soviet countries are that not only did the principles of periodisation inform their annual and long-term calendar planning, but also that this calendar was planned by sports scientists and expert coaches, rather than the administrators working within the sport, as is often the case in Western countries.

Even at the earliest ages relating to the *Training to Win* stage (18 years for boys and 17 years for girls), some performers may be nearing their genetically defined limits. In terms of fitness components, every individual will have a limit or ceiling in relation to development because of their genetic endowment. Obviously, within this stage, the closer the performer is to their limit, the smaller the extent of improvement may be. The reverse would also apply in that the further away the performer was from their ceiling, the greater the opportunity would be to make significant improvements in relation to a specific training load.

When coaches feel that performers are approaching their limits, and smaller performance gains are being demonstrated, greater training loads may be required before even quite modest improvements can be seen. This can be summed up as the law of diminishing returns, which is recognised in sport and exercise physiology literature, and in principles that underpin periodisation. This is not to say that any performer cannot, or will not, continue to improve in any or all of their capabilities during this phase, but the *Training to Win* stage is often known as the phase of *diminishing returns*.

Coaches should be reminded that one aspect of a performer's development cannot be divorced completely from another. Coaches work with individuals and teams, and must be able to adopt a holistic view of them and their development. Also, throughout the development and implementation of a long-term training, competition and recovery plan, especially as the performer matures and becomes more willing and able to contribute, the discussion and negotiation between coach and athlete becomes a key factor. In the spirit of involving performers in their own learning and development, asking them to keep detailed records of their training through the use of a diary, including tapering and peaking, can be a valuable strategy. Through monitoring a detailed training diary, coaches and athletes can assess what aspects of their schedule have been effective and identify any areas where modification seems necessary. Through a thorough evaluation of the training diary, coaches and athletes can make informed judgements about future planning and practice.

To conclude, this approach to planning performer development has been informed by the structure adopted in the former Soviet Union and Eastern European countries. Here, the long seasonal pattern of training of the GPP, leading to the SPP, the PCP and climaxing in the CP has been replaced by shorter phases[1]. The aim of the preparation programme during these shorter phases is to achieve key physical, technical and/or tactical objectives. Within each phase, there is a particular focus on either physical or technical development, and the competitive programme determines the pattern of the phases and their emphases.

[1]Refer to page 37 for definitions of these terms.

Describing all the variations within periodisation, and the appropriateness and effectiveness of these variations, is beyond the scope of this resource. Useful references have been provided for those who are interested to follow up. Coaches will no doubt conclude that the ultimate decision about which type of periodisation to adopt will be a matter for their professional judgement, based on their knowledge of the performer(s), the nature and structure of the sport and the specific context in which they are working.

For the performer to gain optimum benefit from the training and competition programme, the plan must demonstrate total integration of all key aspects of performer development, such as physical and psychological aspects relating to training and performance and the performer's lifestyle. This is no easy task, as it demands rigorous attention to detail. It is of such importance because, if we are to provide a real athlete-centred system and our performers are to achieve at the highest levels, no potential legal or ethically acceptable advantage that a performer may gain should be overlooked.

Do you know the approach to periodisation that is recommended as appropriate by the governing body of your sport?

5.0 KEY MESSAGES FOR COACHING PRACTICE

FUNdamental • Learning to Train • Training to Train • Training to Compete • Training to Win • Retaining

Administrators • Athletes • Coaches • Officials • Parents • Performers • Players • Teachers

5.0 Key Messages for Coaching Practice

The LTAD model described in this resource sets out a useful framework of how adaptation to training programmes and performer trainability progresses throughout the various developmental phases. During the initial *FUNdamental* stage, basic movement skills are emphasised. Nurturing and building overall sports skills is prioritised during the *Learning to Train* stage, while developing the *engine* and sport-specific skills characterise the *Training to Train* stage. These three stages are vitally important in the overall process. By now, coaches will be well aware of the recurrent theme regarding developmental readiness. If there are any key deficiencies in development that are not identified, addressed and rectified within either the *Learning to Train* or *Training to Train* stages, such shortcomings will be very difficult, if not impossible, to correct fully at a later stage.

The *Training to Compete* stage focuses on *fine-tuning the engine* and specific work is undertaken relating to the particular sport, event or positional requirements. Finally, in terms of preparing performers to compete and achieve at the highest levels, the *Training to Win* stage may be characterised as maximising the engine and the specific skills that relate to the sport, event or positional requirements.

"

AFTER I STARTED WORK IN BRITAIN IN 2000, IT BECAME APPARENT TO ME THAT BRITISH AGE GROUP SWIMMERS WERE COMPETING TOO OFTEN AND TRAINING TOO LITTLE. THE LTAD MODEL FOR SWIMMING IS DESIGNED TO ADDRESS THIS FAILING. **"**

Bill Sweetenham
Former National
Performance Director,
British Swimming

5.1 Development Targets

In addition to the aforementioned issue of providing support for high-level performers who have retired from mainstream competition, key issues have been identified in relation to gaps that exist within sport systems, which impair overall development.

The way in which competitive events are planned is perhaps better thought through than previously, but some competitive programmes are still based more on tradition than on an application of scientific and technical principles. This system, and in some cases the complete lack of a systemised approach to competition, will not support optimum training and performance, and may even impair individual development.

> The competitive structure may make or break a performer.
>
> *After I started work in Britain in 2000, it became apparent to me that British Age Group swimmers were competing too often and training too little. The LTAD model for swimming is designed to address this failing.*
>
> **Bill Sweetenham**
> **Former National Performance Director, British Swimming**

The previous chapter concluded with a statement suggesting that talent identification and development may have been a neglected area. In past years, coaching practice, and the administrative structures that support it, may have focused on training and competition to the detriment of structured talent identification and development. Now, national sports agencies and governing bodies of sport seem to have started to address this issue. Centres of excellence and academies should become a welcome focal point for the planning, implementation and evaluation of a structured and coordinated talent identification and development system. However, the success of any such system will depend on the appropriate principles and practices that have been set out in the preceding chapters in relation to the effective implementation of LTAD.

In the UK, our most knowledgeable, experienced and best-qualified coaches do tend to operate almost exclusively with the higher level performers. Lots of money and effort is concentrated at the highest levels, but the message from LTAD is that this will not fully compensate for deficiencies at the early stages of development. Coaches working within the *FUNdamental, Learning to Train* and *Training to Train* stages tend to be either unqualified volunteers (although a number of governing bodies of sport are now addressing this issue) or have a basic Level 1 qualification, or equivalent. The argument that has existed for many years is that the early years of an individual's development are the most crucial and are therefore deserving of high-quality coaching.

The LTAD model described in this resource illustrates that the *Learning to Train* and the *Training to Train* stages are the most critical to long-term individual development. Indeed, it is claimed that this is where we make or break a performer. If the framework that this model provides, and the principles it sets out, are adopted by governing bodies of sport, it may be recognised that coaching at these two early stages demands a coaching workforce that is knowledgeable, experienced and able to relate well to young athletes, responding sensitively to their needs. Suitable coaches will need to be actively recruited, encouraged and deployed to work at these levels. Such individuals need to understand how children develop, not only physically, but also in terms of their cognitive, social and emotional pathways. At various points throughout this resource, it has been suggested that failure to capitalise on potential at the relevant stages cannot be fully compensated for later. It is worth stressing that, if young participants are subjected to ineffective, or even incompetent, coaching during these early stages, it may not be possible to correct fully the problems created during the subsequent *Training to Compete* or *Training to Win* stages.

Further details on the physical, cognitive and emotional development of children are provided in Appendix B.

The quality of support also appears to improve significantly at the higher performance levels. Whereas real quality support mechanisms and structures are needed at the higher levels, the present system of apportioning resources means that developing performers often lack the support they need. Because of such difficulties young participants may encounter during the *FUNdamental, Learning to Train* and *Training to Train* stages, many will never achieve their optimum performance levels or fulfil their true potential. Once again, it must be stressed that no matter how good the support is at the highest levels, this will not compensate for earlier limitations. Centres of excellence, academies and national sport centres provide valuable support to performers, but they will not be able to operate to maximum effect until improvements are made to support structures that encourage and develop performers at earlier training ages.

The focus of training and competitive activities can also create problems. Optimal development will be impaired when there is a high ratio of formal competition to training activities during the earlier stages. This is a particular issue when considering that the preparation of young athletes at earlier stages is often characterised by an emphasis on winning, rather than on the key processes contributing to long-term development. In relation to competition, the lack of an integrated approach to competition systems is evident, mainly at novice and intermediate levels. At the early stages, the ABCs of athletic development do not appear to be addressed in a systematic manner.

Chronological age is used as the main means of classifying young participants when training and competition programmes are being designed, whereas the developmental stage should really be considered. It has been noted that optimum trainability is not addressed at critical or sensitive periods, with only about 2% of coaches using body measurements to identify the onset of PHV[1] and PSV[2] to optimise performer development during periods of accelerated adaptation to training. This is particularly important during the *Training to Train* stage and results in key skills not being introduced to many young performers at the appropriate times, when they are developmentally ready to learn them.

A key implication here is that coach education should address relevant principles of children's growth, development and maturation to a much greater extent, so coaches can provide more developmentally appropriate programmes. Parental education also appears to be neglected in relation to LTAD and coaches will appreciate the valuable role that supportive parents can play – for example, in providing correct nutrition for their growing child.

In terms of the appropriateness of programmes, it is evident that some training regimes developed for adults have been used inappropriately with young participants. This often results in a disproportionately high amount of time being spent on competition and insufficient time devoted to learning and developing the fundamental and sport-specific skills. As well as appreciating and accounting for the differences between adults and children, coaches must understand the training and competition implications of the general physiological, anatomical and developmental differences between males and females.

[1] See page 12.
[2] See page 16.

5.2 LTAD in Practice

Various countries are now showing a significant interest in LTAD. Its potential in terms of providing an appropriate and effective stimulus for change has been recognised by governing bodies of sport, national sport agencies, local authorities and education providers. This change is now beginning to affect:

- the way in which young people are trained and coached
- the variety and balance of sporting activities offered to young people
- the competition, training and recovery pattern within sports
- coach education programmes.

Coaches are urged to ensure they are familiar with developments and initiatives within their own sport(s) and their local communities that are designed to create this more integrated, systematic and progressive system to developing young people in and through sport.

In practice, all coaches working with young people have to concern themselves primarily with the health and well-being of their developing athletes. As highlighted in the introduction, coaches should understand that their remit is in helping young people to develop as individuals and not just to help them develop as future sports performers.

Coaches interested in keeping up to date with current initiatives, programmes and developments within the overall context of LTAD should visit www.sportscoachuk.org for relevant information and specific case studies.

6.0 Summary

Although Balyi's LTAD model has provided the focus for this resource, variations and adaptations have also been identified. The key aspects of the LTAD model that coaches are urged to consider can be summarised as follows:

- Training, competition and recovery programmes should be set in relation to an individual's developmental, rather than chronological, age.
- Optimal windows of trainability should be identified and used.
- The structure of the competition programme should be reviewed to optimise the ratio between competitive events and training.
- The overall system (ie athlete development; competition structures and schedules; coach education and development; resources available at the various levels) needs to be aligned and integrated.

In the future, many more approaches and systems will, undoubtedly, come to prominence and be deserving of our consideration. Coaches need to examine the principles, issues and implications of any such model, rather than simply *buying into* the latest initiative. Whatever future systems, structures or models are proposed, coaches will have an integral role to play in assuring that such systems are implemented to best effect.

Earle (2002) suggests that coaches need to give more thought to their performers' lives beyond sport. Coaches may have a significant influence in terms of helping individuals learn how to balance their academic, social, work and sport commitments. He concludes that producing a vision is relatively easy in comparison with actually making it happen. Coaches play a central role in translating vision into action, which is why it was stated at the start of this resource that your role as a coach has never been more important. Yes, this role has associated challenges and responsibilities, but your commitment to being as excellent a coach as you can be is a good foundation from which to encourage excellence in your performers, so that they strive to be the best they can be.

In aiming to be as good a coach as possible, consideration must be given to the coach education and development implications of implementing any LTAD-type approach effectively. At various points throughout this resource, the issue of the coach's requirements and needs has been raised. If we are to produce a coaching workforce that is up to the challenges of supporting and guiding performers through the LTAD stages, then surely any model of athlete development must be accompanied by an appropriate coach development model. Harrison and Crouch (2002) outlined how the development of athletes and coaches could be seen as complementary (see Figure 9 overleaf).

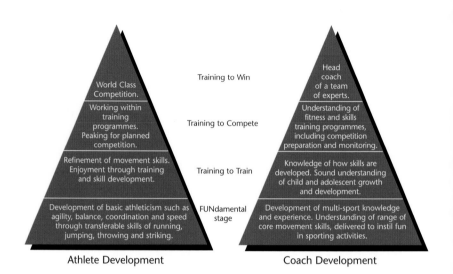

Figure 9: The dual development model for athletes and coaches (Harrison and Crouch, 2002)[1]

As stated in the introduction to this resource, the need to support coach development is now seen as integral to the Government's Sport Strategy. The Government quote in the Preface is part of the following, longer statement:

The Government recognises that coaching is central to the development of sport at every level and we need to make coaching education programmes accessible and widely available.

Department for Culture, Media and Sport, 2001

This recognition of the need for effective coach education, together with the *UK Vision for Sport* (1999) inform the Harrison and Crouch proposal. The characteristics of their model are illustrated in Figure 10 overleaf, where the levels of coaching qualifications (on the vertical axis) are related to the stages of athlete development (horizontal axis).

❝

THE GOVERNMENT RECOGNISES THAT COACHING IS CENTRAL TO THE DEVELOPMENT OF SPORT AT EVERY LEVEL AND WE NEED TO MAKE COACHING EDUCATION PROGRAMMES ACCESSIBLE AND WIDELY AVAILABLE.

❞

Department for Culture, Media and Sport, 2001

[1] Note that this model was proposed before the *Learning to Train* stage was added.

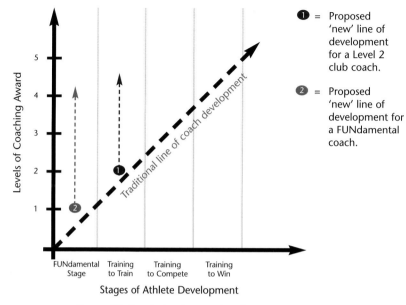

**Figure 10: Coach development pathway
(Harrison and Crouch, 2002)**

The thick, diagonal, dotted line identifies the traditional coach development pathway. In reality, this meant that coaches had to work with more senior and higher level performers in order to access and achieve higher-level coaching awards. The more recent challenge is to provide an alternative pathway in coach development, with coaches being able to progress within the same band or stage. This has been discussed for some time as horizontal progression, rather than the previous vertical progression (although this terminology may be somewhat confusing, as the horizontal progression suggested in the Harrison and Crouch model is actually represented by vertical lines – numbered 1 and 2).

Practising coaches may think that the issue of structuring complementary athlete and coach development frameworks is one that key decision-makers, rather than active coaches, should concern themselves with. However, just as the aim of coaching is to produce independent athletes, any coach education structure must aim to produce independent coaches, who have a similar capability to maximise the support services for their own development at every stage. The message is a simple one: decision-makers may develop models, structures and systems that could be of great benefit to all who participate in sport, but it is the coaches who have the key role of acting on them and making them work in practice.

As a coach, you must be aware of all the support that exists to help you in your own development and you must be able to make informed judgements about your own progression pathway. If you can reflect on, and make appropriate decisions about, your own development, you may be better placed to encourage your performers, at whatever level, to make informed decisions about their development in sport. Coaches translate vision into action and are a key resource in the recruitment, retention and development of athletes. If you perform your job excellently, as well as you can, then you will have a better chance of recruiting more, retaining more and achieving more, at all levels. As stated previously, important responsibilities are associated with this challenge. **Accepting and meeting the challenge is potentially a rich source of satisfaction – but only if we plan for real long-term athlete development and implement appropriate and effective policies, programmes and practices.**

Further details on player/athlete capacities at each stage of the LTAD model are provided in Appendix C.

7.0 References

Balyi, I. (1998a) 'Long-term Planning of Athlete Development – The Training to Train Phase', *FHS*, (1): 8–11.

Balyi, I. (1998b) 'Long-term Planning of Athlete Development – The Training to Compete Phase', *FHS*, (2): 8–11.

Balyi, I. (2002) 'Long-term Athlete Development – the System and Solutions', *FHS*, (14): 6–9.

Balyi, I. and Hamilton, A. (1999a) 'Long-term Planning of Athlete Development – The Training to Win Phase', *FHS*, (3): 7–9.

Balyi, I. and Hamilton, A. (1999b) 'Long-term Planning of Athlete Development – Multiple Periodization, Modelling and Normative Data', *FHS*, (4): 7–9.

Balyi, I. and Hamilton, A. (2003) 'Long-term Athlete Development Update – Trainability in Childhood and Adolescence', *FHS*, (20): 6–8.

Balyi, I. and Way, R. (1995) 'Long-Term Planning of Athlete Development. The Training to Train Phase'. *B.C. Coach*, 2–10.

Balyi, I. and Williams, C. (2009) *Coaching the Young Developing Performer: Tracking Physical Growth and Development to Inform Coaching Programmes*. Leeds: Coachwise Business Solutions. ISBN: 978-1-905540-37-2.

Bar–Or, O. (ed) (1996) *The Child and the Adolescent Athlete*. Oxford: Blackwell Science Ltd. ISBN: 0-865429-04-9.

Blimkie, C.J.R. and Marion, A. (1994) 'Resistance Training during Pre-adolescence: Issues, Controversies and Recommendations', *Coaches Report,* 1 (4): 10–14.

Bompa, T. (1999) *Periodization: Theory and Methodology.* Leeds: Human Kinetics ISBN: 978-0-880118-51-4.

Broomhead, L. (2002) 'Coaching – Progression not Possession', *FHS*, (14): 18–19.

Department for Culture, Media and Sport (2001) *A Sporting Future for All.* London: Department for Culture, Media and Sport.

Drake, I. (2002) 'The Need for Lifestyle Balance', *FHS*, (14): 20–21.

Earle, C. (2002) 'A Framework for the Development of Gifted and Talented Sportspeople in Schools', *FHS*, (14): 10–13.

Fagenbaum, A.D., O'Connell, J., Glover, S., O'Connell, J., Westcott, W.L. (2001) 'Effect of Different Resistance Learning Protocols on Upper Body Strength and Endurance Development in Children', *Journal of Strength and Conditioning Research*, 15 (4): 459–465.

Harrison, P. and Crouch, H. (2002) 'Coaching the Coaches', *FHS*, (14): 26–27.

Malina, R.M. and Bouchard, C. (2004) *Growth, Maturation, and Physical Activity.* Leeds: Human Kinetics Europe. ISBN: 0-880118-82-2.

National Coaching & Training Centre. (2003) *Building Pathways In Irish Sport.* Consultation paper, University of Limerick.

Platonov, V.N. (1988) *L'Entraînement Sportif: Théorie et Méthode.* Paris: Ed EPS.

Prescott, J. (2004) *British Gymnastics Briefing Paper* (unpublished document).

Rushall, B. (1998) 'The Growth of Physical Characteristics in Male and Female Children', *Sports Coach,* 20 (64): 25–27.

Tanner, J.M. (1989) *Foetus into Man: Physical Growth from Conception to Maturity.* Castlemead Publications. ISBN: 0-948555-24-6.

Tomlins, K. (2003) 'Quality Matters', *Hitting the Scene,* (11): 4.

Tschiene, P. ‚Veranderungen in der Structure des Jahnrestainingzyklus', *Die Lehre der Leichtathletik,* 29: 1519–1522.

Viru, A. (1995) *Adaptation in Sports Training.* London: CRC Press. ISBN: 0-849301-71-8.

Viru, A., Loko, J., Volver, A., Laaentos, L., Karelson, K. and Viru, M. (1998) 'Age Periods of Accelerated Improvements of Muscle Strength, Power, Speed and Endurance in the Age Interval 6–18 Years', *Biology of Sport,* 15 (4): 211–227.

sports coach UK produces *Coaching Edge,* the UK's leading coaching magazine, formerly known as *Faster, Higher, Stronger (FHS).* Details of this service are available from:

sports coach UK
114 Cardigan Road
Headingley
Leeds LS6 3BJ
Tel: 0113-274 4802
Fax: 0113-275 5019
Email: coaching@sportscoachuk.org
Website: www.sportscoachuk.org

For subscription information or to purchase back copies of *Coaching Edge* or *FHS,* please call 0113-290 7612.

Appendix A — Developing Key Performance Components

Stage	Strength	Suppleness (Flexibility)	Stamina (Endurance)	Speed	Skill
FUNdamental	• Gains mainly in strength related to body weight. • Training can be introduced at a very early training age – using own body weight, appropriately weighted medicine and Swiss ball exercises for fun. • Swiss ball activities also for core stability and upper/lower body strength.	• Introduce training through enjoyable games. • Should be done five/six times per week if flexibility needs to be improved. • Two/three flexibility training sessions per week or training every other day will maintain existing flexibility levels. • **Extensive** static stretching should be removed from the warm-up as it does not prevent injuries.	• Trainability of aerobic system is good. • Aerobic training in form of fun games with an aerobic component. • Short attention span so presenting a variety of games, one after the other, is ideal.	• First *window* for speed training here. • Training aimed at development of CNS rather than energy system. • Volume of training is very low, but challenging, with activity bursts of less than five seconds.	• Aim to develop physical literacy – agility, balance, coordination and speed (ABCs) through activities designed to improve: running, jumping, throwing, catching, passing, kicking, striking. • Swiss ball activities can help improve balance and the bouncing versions can help improve coordination.
Learning to Train	• Continue with activities that use own body weight. • Large muscle groups to be developed and may want to introduce lifting patterns using light bars.	• No specific guidelines apart from continuing to improve the component by well-sequenced training.	• No specific guidelines apart from continuing to improve the component by well-sequenced training.	• By end of this stage, aim to be working on short sprints, acceleration and reaction speed.	• This is the major skill learning stage, so skill development must be emphasised during this period. • Basic skills acquired in *FUNdamental* stage should be developed.

Stage	Strength	Suppleness (Flexibility)	Stamina (Endurance)	Speed	Skill
Training to Train	• Strength training two/three times per week, up to 30 mins maximum. • Onset of PHV determines extent and frequency of training. • Olympic lifting techniques with light bars can be introduced with the onset of PHV. • Mastering these techniques helps prevent injury if working with free weights. • Start free weight training earlier with athletes who have early onset of PHV and later for those who have late onset of PHV.	• Flexibility should be monitored carefully. • Static stretching and PNF complemented, if required, by active isolated stretching (a dynamic stretch with an isolated muscle or muscle group). • A separate session devoted to stretching is recommended. • Dynamic mobility and preparation routines should replace static stretching in warm-ups.	• Group according to biological maturation rather than chronological age. • Most of the aerobic training should be non-weight-bearing aerobic activities, such as swimming and cycling, to help prevent injuries.	• Second speed *window* here. • CNS training still very important. • Anaerobic alactic power and anaerobic alactic capacity interval training should be introduced to girls during the first part of this stage and to boys during the second part. • Appropriate loads – intensity, frequency, duration must be ensured. • Linear, lateral and multi-directional speed trained by proper sequencing of speed work with other training activities. • Speed work done all year round and within a session, after the warm-up, so no fatigue and volume is low.	• Revisit movement and technical skills because of growth during adolescence. • Be patient and sensitive with athletes during, and immediately after, growth spurts. • Different parts of the body grow at different rates – this may temporarily have an adverse effect on the performance of skills.
Training to Compete	• In principle, performers are now fully trainable in all five components; diagnostic tests will identify individual needs. • Strengths and weaknesses of performers will inform decision-making regarding training priorities and programmes. • Optimal sequencing of training activities within micro- and mesocycles needed to minimise interference among the five components.				

Stage	Strength	Suppleness (Flexibility)	Stamina (Endurance)	Speed	Skill
	• All capacities fully established – focus of training shifts to optimising performance. • Diagnostic testing determines priorities. • Reduced training volumes during competitions mean that established qualities and capacities need to be maintained. • Recovery protocols and frequent short rest periods or prophylactic breaks implemented to help prevent burnout.				
Training to Win	• Strength training every 7–10 days.		• Aerobic training two/three times per week. • Recovery runs of 30 mins at 70% maximum heart rate after competitive games/events or hard practice help to remove the by-products of exertion and can contribute to maintenance of aerobic system. • Non-weight-bearing activities (cycling, swimming, aqua-aerobics) can lessen potential for injury and provide variety to break monotony of normal training routine.		

Appendix B Physical, Mental/Cognitive and Emotional Development in Children

Tables of the Stages of Athlete Development

Characteristics of Physical, Mental/Cognitive and Emotional Development

FUNdamental	Learning to Train	Training to Train	Training to Compete	Training to Win
Late Childhood		Late Puberty		
	Early Puberty		Early Adulthood	

Table 1a
Physical Development Characteristics and its Implications

1. LATE CHILDHOOD FUNdamental Stage

Basic Characteristics	General Consequences: Performance Capabilities and Limitations	Implications for the Coach
Larger muscle groups are more developed than smaller ones	The child is more skilful in gross movements involving large muscle groups rather than precise coordinated movements involving the interaction of many smaller muscles	General basic skills should be developed during this phase
The size of the heart is increasing in relation to the rest of the body. The cardiovascular system is still developing	Endurance capacity of the young participants, however, is more than adequate for most activities (little aerobic machines)	Short duration anaerobic activities to be planned (alactic); endurance must be developed through play and games (lack of attention span for continuous work)
Ligamentous structures are becoming stronger, but the ends of the bones are still cartilaginous and continue to calsify	The body is very susceptible to injuries through excessive stress or heavy pressure	Individual progression in hopping, bounding, use of own body weight, appropriately weighted medicine ball exercises (neural recruitment)
Basic motor patterns become more refined towards the end of the phase and the balance mechanism in the inner ear is gradually maturing	There is great improvement in speed, agility, balance, coordination and flexibility toward the end of this phase	Specific activities and games should emphasise coordination and kinaesthetic sense, gymnastics, diving, athletics field events
During this phase, girls develop coordination skills faster than boys but generally there are no differences between boys and girls	Sex differences are not of any great consequences at this stage in development	Training and playing together should be emphasised at this age and phase

Table 1b
Mental/Cognitive Development Characteristics and its Implications

Basic Characteristics	General Consequences: Performance Capabilities and Limitations	Implications for the Coach
Attention span is short and children are very much action oriented. Memory is developing in a progressive way	Young performers cannot sit and listen for longer periods of time	Use short, clear and simple instructions. Children want to move and participate in action
Children in this phase have very limited reasoning ability. Later in the phase there is a growing capability for more abstract thought	Children are generally leader oriented – they love to be led!	Coaches should adopt a 'follow me' or 'follow the leader' approach and ensure that all activities are fun and well planned
The repetition of activities is greatly enjoyed. Young children improve their abilities through experience	Children do not learn the skills correctly just by trial and error alone	Coaches must be able to provide appropriate demonstrations of basic skills required at this level and constructive, corrective feedback
Imagination is blossoming	Experimentation and creativity should be encouraged	While playing and practising, encourage input (opinion) from the children. They love to try new things and are ready to try almost anything

Table 1c
Emotional Development Characteristics and its Consequences

Basic Characteristics	General Consequences: Performance Capabilities and Limitations	Implications for the Coach
The child's concept of self is developing at this phase by experiences and comments from others	Youngsters perceive these experiences as a form of self-evaluation. 'I am a good person if I do well, I'm a bad person if I do poorly'	The coach needs to provide **positive reinforcement** on a regular basis. This will provide strong motivation to continue with the activity
Children like to be the centre of focus and attention	When situation becomes threatening, they quickly lose confidence	Select technical and tactical activities in which success is virtually guaranteed, gradual progress from simple to complex
The influence of peers becomes a very strong driving force behind all activities	Acceptance into the peer group often depends upon one's capabilities in physical skills and activities	At this phase the coach must be capable of properly assessing the basic skills and providing a varied repertoire of practical opportunities for technical and tactical development and improvement
The child begins to understand the need for rules and structure	They can understand and play simple games with simple rules and will tend to question rules and expect thoughtful answers	Participation and **enjoyment** to be emphasised versus winning. **Focus on the processes not on the outcome (and have lots of FUN)!**

Table 2a
Physical Development Characteristics and its Implications

Basic Characteristics	General Consequences: Performance Capabilities and Limitations	Implications for the Coach
Significant proportional changes occur in bone, muscle and fat tissue	During growth spurts, adaptation is influenced by sudden changes of body proportions	Monitor training carefully and individualise training to ensure adaptation
Girls begin their growth spurt between the ages of 12.5–14 years, boys between 12.5–15 years. Girls attain a maximum rate of growth at an average age of 11, boys at an average age of 14 years	Early in this phase, girls are faster and stronger than boys, later in the phase boys are becoming faster and stronger than girls	Chronological age and sex may not be the most appropriate ways to group young performers
Primary and secondary sex characteristics manifest themselves during this period. The normal range for onset of menarche for girls can be anywhere from 10–16 years	After the onset of menarche, iron levels of girls should be monitored regularly	Situations when fear, guilt or anxiety brought about by sexual development should be avoided
Smaller muscle groups are becoming more developed	Speed, agility and coordination are still improving rapidly during this stage	With the improvement of fine motor movement, all basic technical skills to be mastered. Children should learn how to train during this phase, including physical, technical, tactical and ancillary capabilities

75

Table 2a (continued)
Physical Development Characteristics and its Implications

Basic Characteristics	General Consequences: Performance Capabilities and Limitations	Implications for the Coach
During this developmental phase the various parts of the body do not grow at the same rate. The growth rate of the legs and arms will reach a peak prior to that of the trunk	A change in the centre of gravity, length of limbs and core strength will determine the content and structure of training	Some of the skills may have to be re-learned or refined again, since the growth of limbs will impact on the technique
A significant increase in red blood cells occurs during this phase, especially in boys, due to the male hormone, testosterone	The oxygen transportation system is still developing and aerobic endurance is continuing to increase	The increase in body mass requires more structured aerobic training. Only short duration of anaerobic activities are recommended
The central nervous system (CNS) is almost fully developed	Agility, balance and coordination is fully trainable	Use appropriate warm-up activities to promote development of CNS

Table 2b
Mental/Cognitive Development Characteristics and its Implications

Basic Characteristics	General Consequences: Performance Capabilities and Limitations	Implications for the Coach
Abstract thinking becomes more firmly established	Decision-making through more complex technical training should be introduced	Decision-making on tactical and strategic solutions should be based upon the skill level of the performer
Young performers develop a new form of egocentric thought. Much emphasis is placed upon self-identity	This may result in a strong fear of failure	Create optimum learning environment, match skill and drill levels. Introduce simple coping strategies, concentration skills and mental imagery
Young performers are eager to perfect their skills	Individual specific direction and structure in the learning process is required. A variety of methods to measure success are important to maintain motivation	Positive reinforcement is imperative. The difference between the physical and mental development can vary to a great extent. The coach must be particularly careful not to pick the early developers and neglect or deselect the late developers. The coach's ability to provide demonstration of specific skills is important. Audiovisual material and video feedback will help to create a mental image

Table 2c
Emotional Development and its Implications

Basic Characteristics	General Consequences: Performance Capabilities and Limitations	Implications for the Coach
The peer group exerts a tremendous influence on behaviour	Values and attitudes are being created and reinforced by the group	The coach should exercise strong direction and supervision. A role model for young athletes at this phase is very important
During this phase performers are capable of cooperating and accepting some responsibility	Some performers may be less responsible, mainly due to a fear of failure	Coach must have an open communication with the performers
Tension generally exists between adults and adolescent	Communication channels should be kept open by the adult, as all teenagers need help even though they do not recognise the need, or seem grateful for the help	Coach is usually better accepted than other adults and should always attempt to foster two-way communication. Young performers should have an input into decision-making processes
It is important for young athletes, at this developmental level, to be able to display tenderness, admiration and appreciation	Deprivation of these qualities often leads to exaggerated and/or unacceptable behaviour	Early maturers often become leaders and excel in physical performance. Coaches must not play favourites as this can have negative effects on other participants' development
Physical, mental and emotional maturity do not necessarily develop at the same rate	Feelings of confusion or anxiety may exist as a result	The coach's communication skills and understanding are important in these regards
There is a desire to have friends of the opposite sex	Social activities are important events for this age group	Co-educational activities are recommended

Table 3a
Physical Development Characteristics and its Implications

Basic Characteristics	General Consequences: Performance Capabilities and Limitations	Implications for the Coach	3. LATE PUBERTY Training to Train and Training to Compete Stages
The circulatory and respiratory system reach maturity	These systems are generally capable of giving maximum output	Aerobic and anaerobic systems can be trained for maximum output. Full sport-specific energy system training should be implemented	
Increases in height and weight gradually lessen. Stabilisation occurs in the muscular system	Muscles have grown to their mature size but muscular strength continues to increase reaching its peak in the late 20s	Strength training can be maximised to improve overall strength development. Neuromuscular training should be optimised during this phase	
Skeletal maturation continues in males and females	Connective tissues are still strengthening	Progressive overloading in training should be continued	
By the age of 17, girls have generally reached adult proportions, whereas boys do not reach such proportions until several years later	Proportionally girls gain more weight than boys during this phase	Aerobic training for girls to be optimised. Also coaches should be aware of how to deal with weight gain and its impact on physique. Athletes should learn how to compete including technical, tactical and ancillary capabilities	

Table 3b
Mental/Cognitive Development Characteristics and its Implications

Basic Characteristics	General Consequences: Performance Capabilities and Limitations	Implications for the Coach
Generally, by the age of 16, the brain has reached its adult size, but continues to mature neurologically for several more years	Performers can cope with multiple strategies and tactics, particularly near the end of the phase	Coaches should ensure the refinement of all technical and tactical skills
Critical thinking is developing well during this phase	The capability to self-analyse and correct is developing	Decision-making should be developed further through technical, tactical development

Table 3c
Emotional Development Characteristics and its Implications

Basic Characteristics	General Consequences: Performance Capabilities and Limitations	Implications for the Coach
Peer group influence is still a powerful force	Independent decision-making and leadership skills are becoming more developed	Performers should be given the opportunity to develop through participation in appropriate leadership or responsible role, (ie team captain, athlete representative, etc), but strong direction and discipline must be maintained
Performers are searching for a stable, balanced self-image	Self-esteem is still very susceptible to successes and failures. Coping techniques are useful	Positive evaluation of performances and positive reinforcement are imperative
Activities and interaction with the opposite sex may play a strong part during this phase	Male performers must be aware that female performers now face an issue of femininity versus sport development. Female performers must be aware that male athletes may now face a problem of relating performance to masculinity	Facilitate the recognition of the former issues through education and club programmes

Table 4a
Physical Development Characteristics and its Implications

4. EARLY ADULTHOOD Training to Compete and Training to Win Stages	Basic Characteristics	General Consequences: Performance Capabilities and Limitations	Implications for the Coach
	Physiologically the body reaches maturity during this phase	All physiological systems are fully trainable. Physical training programmes should employ the most advanced techniques and sports science information to facilitate maximum adaptation and minimise injuries	Ensure that all muscle groups and body alignments are well balanced and complemented with optimum flexibility ranges. State-of-the-art testing and monitoring programme to used. Overtraining and overstress should be carefully monitored
	Final skeletal maturation in females occurs at about 19–20 years and in males about three years later		Regular specialist medical monitoring should be organised with additional blood tests for female performers (anaemia)

Table 4b
Mental/Cognitive Development Characteristics and its Implications

Basic Characteristics	General Consequences: Performance Capabilities and Limitations	Implications for the Coach
Neurologically the brain matures at about 19–20 years of age	Performers are capable of self-analysing, correcting and refining skills. Athletes can analyse and conceptualise all facets of their sport	Winning becomes more of a focus
	Well-developed information processing skills improve the performers' ability to visualise verbal instructions	Principles of adult learning should be implemented at this level
There is a complete understanding and acceptance of the need for rules, regulations and structure	However, the young adult must perceive the rules and structure as being clearly defined and fair	Involve the performers in decision-making and planning of team or group activities

Table 4c
Emotional Development Characteristics and Its Implications

Basic Characteristics	General Consequences: Performance Capabilities and Limitations	Implications for the Coach
There is a need to be self-directed and independent	The performers are ready to assume responsibility and accept the consequences of their actions	Goal-setting should be strongly emphasised to give definite direction and purpose to the athletes' overall programme
Self-actualisation and self-expression are important	Performers may exhibit an increased desire to fulfil their potential and 'be the best they can be'	The athletes need to be treated as adults, with respect. Direction and structure provided by the coach is still important
Major decisions on career, education and lifestyle are a priority at some point in this phase	Major changes in interests, hobbies and physical activities occur during this phase	Professional guidance should be made available, considering off-season and educational pursuits
Generally, interactions with the opposite sex continue to be a strong priority, with lasting relationships developing	Enthusiasm and commitment to sport may be adversely affected because of peer group pressure and conflicting priorities	Athletes must have ample opportunities for independent social interaction

Appendix C Statement of Player/Athlete Capabilities at Each Stage of the LTAD Model

FUNdamental Aim: Fun and participation. Learn all fundamental movement skills	Learning to Train Aim: Fun and participation. Learn all fundamental sports skills	Training to Train Aim: Optimise fitness preparation and sport, individual and position-specific training
Physical • General overall development and mobility • Running, jumping, throwing, Agility, Balance, Coordination, Speed (ABCs) • Develop speed, power and endurance through FUN games • Develop linear, lateral and multi-directional speed • Medicine ball, Swiss ball and own-body exercises for strength	**Physical** • Continue to develop ABCs • Continue to develop speed, power and endurance through fun games • Medicine ball, Swiss ball and own-body exercises for strength as well as hopping/bounding exercises • Basic flexibility exercises • Warm-up and stretching	**Physical** • Emphasis on general and balanced physical conditioning • Aerobic training prioritised after onset of Peak Height Velocity (PHV) • Strength training prioritised in females after PHV and with the onset of menarche • Strength training prioritised in males 12–18 months after PHV and flexibility training • Shoulder, elbow, core, spine and ankle stability. Frequent musculoskeletal evaluations during PHV
Mental • Positive attitude to sport • Confidence • Concentration • Achieve success and receive positive reinforcement	**Mental** • Introduction to mental preparation • Understanding of the role of practice • Perseverance • Confidence • Concentration • Achieve success and receive positive reinforcement	**Mental** • Goal-setting (short and medium term) • Imagery (practising and improving technique and self-confidence) • Relaxation (deep breathing) • Patience and control • Concentration • Continue positive reinforcement

FUNdamental Aim: Fun and participation. Learn all fundamental movement skills	**Learning to Train** Aim: Fun and participation. Learn all fundamental sports skills	**Training to Train** Aim: Optimise fitness preparation and sport, individual and position-specific training
Technical • Basic movement skills: proper running, jumping and throwing techniques • Modified skills of different sports • Use of appropriate footwear and clothing • Knowledge of the basics of equipment	**Technical** • Strong emphasis on skill development • Fundamental skills progressively refined, combined and elaborated upon to more sport-specific skills • Practise skills	**Technical** • Further develop and consolidate sport-specific skills • Individualisation to address strengths and weaknesses
Tactical • Introduction to simple rules and ethics of sport • Basic movement and game concepts	**Tactical** • Modified and small-sided games • Key game principles	**Tactical** • Early stages of tactical preparation • Basic and intermediate team/individual tactics

Training to Compete Aim: Optimise fitness preparation and sport, individual and position-specific training	**Training to Win** Aim: Maximise fitness preparation and sport, individual and position-specific skills as well as performance	**Retirement/ Retaining** Aim: To enjoy a healthy, active lifestyle and retain performers/athletes for coaching, administration roles etc
Physical • Sport, position and individual specific intensive physical conditioning • Shoulder, elbow, core, spine and ankle stability • Optimum preparation: tapering and peaking	**Physical** • Maintenance and possible improvement of physical capacities with a view to maximising performance • Shoulder, elbow, core, spine and ankle stability • All aspects individualised • Frequent 'prophylactic' (rest/recuperation) breaks	**Physical** • Keep active through sports participation • Endurance training • Strength training • Flexibility training

Training to Compete	Training to Win	Retaining
Aim: Optimise fitness preparation and sport, individual and position-specific training	**Aim:** Maximise fitness preparation and sport, individual and position-specific skills as well as performance	**Aim:** To enjoy a healthy, active lifestyle and retain performers/athletes for coaching, administration roles etc

Mental
- Focus and thought control – self-talk/verbal cues (dealing with distractions and negative thoughts)
- Goal-setting (long term)
- Performance routines and pre-competition preparation. Imagery (competition, different situations/problems, practising strategies)
- Anxiety control and relaxation (eg Progressive Muscle Relaxation)
- Personal responsibility and involvement in decision-making

Mental
- Well-developed, refined and individualised mental skills and routines
- Refocusing plans/coping strategies
- Will-to-win/drive
- Concentration/focus
- Independent decision-making
- Capable of teamwork and taking advice

Mental
- Relaxation
- Readjustment to non-competitive environment

Technical
- Proficiency in basic sports skills
- Sport-specific technical and playing skills under competitive conditions and at high intensity
- Individualisation of skills: 'personal style'
- Consistency and control
- Competition-simulation training

Technical
- Complete the refinement of sport-specific skills
- Event or competition-specific training skills are 'automatic'/'second nature'
- Ability to improvise with skills

Technical
- Retain skills or develop new ones

Tactical
- Event and position-specific tactical preparation
- Principles of attack and defence
- Ability to plan and assess competition
- Adaptation to different situations
- Observe and adapt to opponents

Tactical
- Develop effective competitive strategies
- Adapt strategies to situations
- Model all possible aspects of performance in training
- Play to strengths, exploit weaknesses of opponents

Tactical
- Retain recreational involvement

FUNdamental Aim: Fun and participation. Learn all fundamental movement skills	Learning to Train Aim: Fun and participation. Learn all fundamental sports skills	Training to Train Aim: Optimise fitness, preparation and sport, individual and position-specific training
Lifestyle • Involvement in multi-sports • Learn safety	**Lifestyle** • Involvement in multi-sports • Inclusion of sport in lifestyle • Participation in complementary sports	**Lifestyle** • Rest and recovery • Nutrition/ hydration • Training and performance diary/log • Time management • Introduction to planning and periodisation
Personal • Enjoyment/fun • Fair play • Positive attitude • Teamwork/ interaction skills	**Personal** • Understanding of changes which puberty will bring • Accepts discipline and structure • Understands the relationship between effort and outcome • Teamwork/ interaction skills	**Personal** • Interpersonal skills and learning to work in team environment • Positive communication • Discipline and personal responsibility • Awareness of Peak Height Velocity (PHV) and windows of trainability
Physical activity 5–6 times per week	**Sport-specific training three times per week, participation in other sports three times per week**	**Sport-specific training 6–9 times per week**

Training to Compete Aim: Optimise fitness preparation and sport, individual and position-specific training	Training to Win Aim: Maximise fitness preparation and sport, individual and position-specific skills as well as performance	Retaining Aim: To enjoy a healthy, active lifestyle and retain performers/athletes for coaching, administration roles etc
Lifestyle • Individualisation of ancillary support systems • Refined self-monitoring • Plan career/sport options • Increased knowledge on hydration and nutrition • Preparation for different environments (eg heat/cold/rain/altitude) • Injury prevention and recovery	**Lifestyle** • Increased knowledge of all areas • Rest and relaxation. Frequent breaks • Well-developed self-monitoring • Well-developed and integrated support network/structure • Career/sport planning sustained	**Lifestyle** • Pursue personal and family goals more strongly • Pursue further education/career development • Possible engagement in administration, coaching, media/PR • Seek transition support, if required
Personal • Continued personal development • Integration of sport, career and life goals • Economic and independence issues addressed	**Personal** • Full integration of sport, career and life goals	**Personal** • Reset goals
Sport-specific technical, tactical and fitness training 9–12 times per week	**Sport-specific technical, tactical and fitness training 9–15 times per week**	**Physical activity 3–6 times per week**

The material in Appendices A, B and C is taken from *Building Pathways in Irish Sport,* Consultation paper, University of Limerick. Some, generally minor, alterations have been made to the text.

sports coach UK
The National Coaching Foundation
Great Coaches...Great Sport

Mission Statement

sports coach UK is dedicated to guiding the development and implementation of a coaching system, recognised as a world leader, for all coaches at every level in the UK.

We will work with our partners to achieve this, by promoting:

- professional and ethical values
- inclusive and equitable practice
- agreed national standards of competence as a benchmark at all levels
- a regulated and licensed structure
- recognition, value and appropriate funding and reward
- a culture and structure of innovation, constant renewal and continuous professional development (CPD).